TESTIMONIALS

"Brenda has generously wrapped her personal and professional experiences, extensive research, knowledge, and love into *Courageously Authentic*. Her own story, along with the stories of the amazing women she has coached, shows us that we are not alone on this journey and that achieving authenticity while loving ourselves is truly possible. The exercises in this book offer tools to create a personalized path to self-discovery, healing, and fearlessly embracing and revealing our authentic selves. Regardless of your background, *Courageously Authentic* will resonate with you—all you need is a journal, a pen, and the readiness to change."

–*Trish B.*

"At some point in our lives, especially as women over 40, many of us feel stuck and disconnected from our passion and purpose. *Courageously Authentic* was truly transformative for me, reigniting my sense of self and direction. It moved me from an unconscious victim mindset to embracing self-love and unconditional acceptance. From the first page, Brenda's insights resonated deeply, offering relatable experiences and posing the tough questions we often avoid. Guided by the book's exercises, I acknowledged and healed my past, which opened the door to a brighter, more fulfilling future. Facing my truths with honesty, courage, and accountability led to life-changing results. Now, I approach life with renewed confidence, guided by integrity, truth, and authenticity. *Courageously Authentic* isn't just a guide for those feeling lost and unfulfilled—it's a transformative journey back to reclaiming your true, vibrant self."

–*Stacy M.*

"This book is like nothing I've read before! Brenda has gathered a variety of stories and woven them together in a way that you can relate to and will be amazed by! With each chapter, she guides you down a path you may not have realized you needed to travel in order to reach a destination you may not have known was possible. The coaching tools, principles, and practices she shares are simple to use yet deeply transformative, empowering individuals to achieve lasting and meaningful changes in their lives."

–Kari W.

"***Courageously Authentic*** brings forth Brenda's wealth of life's wisdom and guidance to assist you in becoming your authentic self. Her stories and exercises brilliantly assist and inspire inner strength with love and compassion for yourself and who you are meant to be. No matter where you are on your life's journey, this book guides you to reach your highest authentic potential and find the truth of who you are with love, compassion, self-acceptance, grace, and ease."

–Deb B.

"Brenda has conveyed deep, thought-provoking knowledge, principles, exercises, and stories in this heartfelt and integrative book. With profound specificity, she outlines a True Heart True Mind version of safely diving into the Unknown. Her graceful approach takes the reader on a rewarding journey into the depths of their consciousness, empowering core integration back to wholeness and encouraging them to courageously embrace the life they desire with fearless authenticity."

–DyAnn S.

Courageously Authentic

BRENDA L. HUKEL

Copyright © 2025 Brenda L. Hukel

All rights reserved. No part of this book may be reproduced by any mechanical, photographic, or electronic process, or in the form of a phonographic recording; nor may it be stored in a retrieval system, transmitted, or otherwise be copied for public or private use—other than for "fair use" as brief quotations embodied in articles and reviews—without prior written permission of the author. The author does not authorize or grant permission to upload or use any portion of this book for artificial intelligence use or purposes.

The author of this book does not dispense medical advice or prescribe the use of any technique as a form of treatment for physical, emotional, or medical problems without the advice of a physician, either directly or indirectly. The intent of the author is only to offer information of a general nature to help you in your quest for emotional well-being. In the event you use any of the information in this book for yourself, the author and the publisher assume no responsibility for your actions.

Note that some names and personal details in the stories within this book have been changed to protect the privacy of those involved. Some stories are also composites of women the author has coached.

MINDSTIR MEDIA

Published by MindStir Media, LLC
45 Lafayette Rd | Suite 181| North Hampton, NH 03862 | USA
1.800.767.0531 | www.mindstirmedia.com

Printed in the United States of America.
ISBN-13: 978-1-962987-86-8

First printing edition 2025

Contents

Dedications vii

Foreword by Dr. Reginald L. Woods, LCPC ix

A Letter to All the Women Who Are Ready to Awaken xi

Section 1: Meeting Your Shadow

Introduction: The Day I Became Invisible xiii

Chapter 1: What's Happening to Me? 1

Chapter 2: Breaking the Ego's Spell:
               Freeing Our Beliefs from Fear of Change 11

Chapter 3: Who Owns Your Belief System? 23

Section 2: Dancing With Your Shadow

Chapter 4: Unmasking Impostor Syndrome 47

Chapter 5: Staying Asleep: The Hidden Cost of Victimhood 71

Chapter 6: The Vibrational Dance of Light and Dark Frequencies 85

Section 3: Releasing Your Shadow

Chapter 7: The Sacred Bonds of Soul Contracts.................................. 95

Chapter 8: Liberation Through Forgiveness:
　　　　　　Embracing the Power of Letting Go 109

Chapter 9: The Path to Awakening 123

Section 4: Awakening The Consciousness Within

Chapter 10: The Conscious Truth About the Hidden Ego 141

Chapter 11: Fear-less Authenticity 147

Chapter 12: Ascending to Christ Consciousness:
　　　　　　　Returning to Wholeness 159

About the Author 173

A Message from the Author 174

References 175

Resources 177

Dedications

This book is dedicated to all the remarkable women ready to awaken their consciousness, embrace fearless authenticity, and transform their lives.

To my devoted and loving husband, Steve, your love and belief in me have been the guiding light on this incredible journey. Your unwavering support and inspiration were instrumental in realizing this dream—to break free from the confines of my corporate job and pursue my lifelong aspiration of writing this book. Thank you for standing by me every step of the way, for being my rock, my inspiration, and my greatest champion. This book stands as a testament to our love and your unwavering confidence in my abilities. It's as much yours as it is mine.

I extend my deepest gratitude to DyAnn Suares, my cherished friend, dedicated mentor, and self-mastery coach at BHN Awareness, LLC. Your profound guidance and unwavering support were invaluable during my healing journey as I transitioned from ego to heart consciousness, rediscovering and embracing an authentic way of life that realigned me with my true self. Your influence has been truly transformative, and I am forever grateful for your wisdom, guidance, and friendship.

To my long-time, trusted, and loyal friend, Debra Baron, I express my heartfelt gratitude for all the support, encouragement, and time you devoted to me throughout my writing journey. Your

DEDICATIONS

friendship, insightful feedback, and generous time empowered me to express my thoughts freely and openly. Your unwavering belief in me, along with your wisdom and kindness, has been invaluable. Thank you for being an integral part of this journey.

Foreword

Brenda has been a friend, student, and inspiration to me for over thirty years. We met when we both held positions in Human Resources in Missouri, and our paths continued to cross at corporate functions. I became her mentor as we shared the many challenges of our jobs, lives, and experiences. These exchanges continue to this day.

I have enjoyed years of thought-provoking interactions with Brenda and have watched her grow into a strong, independent woman who has impacted thousands of lives with her coaching style. She has an innate ability to provide the spiritual knowledge and wisdom that encourages others to heal, reclaim their lives, and be fearlessly authentic.

Although Brenda's journey has been filled with great trials and tribulations, her persistent commitment to God's grace and truth has been an overriding theme that she demonstrates in her personal, professional, and spiritual life, which has led to many triumphs and testimonies. This internal strength has empowered her to remain steadfast and immovable, allowing her to keep her focus when others around her have lost theirs. (Brenda uses the word "God" throughout the book, but please feel free to substitute whatever word for the divine you prefer.)

Brenda refused to let adversity control her life, even when tested beyond the imaginable. Instead, by giving herself a strong dose of self-awareness, she learned a valuable principle: when you realize that something or someone is preventing you from achieving your goals, you must first look inside yourself to find out what's really limiting your forward progress. If we are transparent with ourselves, we will see the culprit every time we look in the mirror.

FOREWORD

Brenda shares her journey and the journeys of other women throughout the pages of this book. She generously provides the tools and spiritual principles she used herself and with others she coached, witnessing remarkable transformations. Brenda guides you on a deep self-exploration to release the fear that paralyzes you from having the courage to change your life due to unhealed trauma, outdated belief systems, childhood conditioning, and societal and cultural demands.

Our savior has reminded us, "In this world, you will have trouble. But take heart! I have overcome the world" (John 16:33 NIV).

If patience is truly a virtue, then Brenda Hukel is one of the most admirable people you will ever encounter! She discloses many examples of patience for you in the following pages.

In this book, you will find answers and resolutions to the issues holding you back and preventing you from living the life you were born to live. If you seek instruction on how to thrive through adversity, this book is for you!

RLW
Dr. Reginald L. Woods, LCPC
Retired HR Executive and Leadership Advocate

A Letter to All the Women Who Are Ready to Awaken

This message is for all the beautiful women ready to stop surviving and start thriving. To transform your life and break out of the old, outdated belief patterns that keep you feeling insecure, unworthy, and paralyzed with fear. It's for those who desire to live fearlessly authentic and return to their true selves.

In this book, I will take you on a journey to explore the impact of your outdated definitions and interpretations of your beliefs and conditioned mindset that originated from childhood and molded your life. Like you, the women you'll read about on these pages lost their way and had a burning desire to rediscover their passion, purpose, and happiness after years of dedicating their lives to everyone but themselves. By using the tools, principles, and exercises I'll provide you as you continue reading, they were able to surrender the invisible masks they hid behind for survival so that they could unveil their true identity—who they are on a soul level. You will be able to do the same.

We will explore the different levels of consciousness and how the belief of staying asleep—an unconscious victim—has served as an illusion of safety. We'll delve deep into the shadows, the sacred bonds of soul contracts, and the liberation of forgiveness and letting go. You'll learn how the universal laws can bring you freedom, joy, and harmony as you courageously step into your power and begin your healing journey to living a conscious life.

You'll discover the power of aligning with Christ Consciousness and break free of the constraints from people, society, and cultural demands. You'll bask in the energy of love and compassion for yourself and others by healing your heart and choosing your life of preference.

I'll share the heartwarming stories of the women in this book, who emerged from the Dark Night of the Soul, embarked on spiritual healing journeys, and reawakened. They took back their power and reclaimed their lives. They learned to love themselves unconditionally, applying their inherent wisdom, transforming their ego mind, and transitioning to conscious living.

Allow me the privilege to guide you on this spiritual journey as you immerse yourself in the stories, principles, and tools on these pages. Be gentle as you permit yourself to reflect, feel, and begin your healing journey to transcend from ego consciousness to heart consciousness, integrating the energy of the highest frequency of all—unconditional love—as you return to wholeness.

You are a beautiful and remarkable individual. Isn't it time to reveal your true self to the world and embrace authenticity fearlessly? It's time for you to be true to yourself.

Introduction

THE DAY I BECAME INVISIBLE

Imagine you've been invited to a formal masquerade ball. You arrive in a black lace chiffon gown, and you style your hair in an elegant French twist. Your nails are perfectly manicured, and your makeup is flawless. You know you look stunning.

But you feel a pang of nervousness in your stomach as you walk into the large ballroom full of people. You look around at all the women dressed in exquisite gowns, and suddenly, that pang of nervousness turns into full-fledged fear. You want to turn around and run home. Your negative thoughts flood your consciousness, and you wonder why you thought you would ever fit in with this caliber of people. You stand frozen for a moment, hoping to slip out without being noticed. You turn to leave and see a table full of ornate masquerade masks. You feel a hand grasp your elbow, and before being whisked away to the dance floor, you grab a mask and place it over your face. As the song ends and another begins, you switch to a different dance partner, but not before changing your mask.

You continue to do this throughout the night, hiding behind multiple masks because you fear others will know you don't belong there if you reveal your true identity. When the night ends, you place all the masks back on the table and return to the safety of your home, where you can just be you.

This metaphor represents what so many of us do. We wear multiple invisible masks throughout the day to fit in and be accepted, validated, or loved by our families, coworkers, friends, society, or social circles. We believe it's easier to pretend to be what others expect so that we can avoid the pain of judgment, rejection, or ridicule. We become a master at this game.

Then, the day comes when we look in the mirror and don't recognize the person looking back at us. And we think to ourselves, "What happened to me? I don't even know who I am anymore or what makes me happy." We feel so emotionally, physically, and spiritually exhausted that we don't know what to do or where to go. Sound familiar?

Maybe you, too, have felt invisible—uncomfortable in your skin. Ask yourself: How many daily roles do you perform that don't reflect your true authentic self? Do you hide behind an invisible mask that provides a false sense of security? Do you stay invisible because it feels safer?

In my more than thirty years in the Human Resources and Organizational Development profession, I coached thousands of people and watched countless numbers of them suffer from childhood conditioning and life experiences that kept them paralyzed. I've seen fear, shame, and childhood trauma stop them from changing their life to live their desired life. I've witnessed people stay in toxic relationships, jobs, work cultures, and friendships because they believed that's what they deserved or because they didn't possess the courage to change. And I've seen people remain victims. As dysfunctional as their life may have been, it was familiar to them.

That's why I decided to write this book. On these pages, you'll discover how the power of our minds can create illusions so real that they form beliefs—whether consciously or unconsciously—that we hold as truths. You'll also learn how our lives mirror our belief systems by attracting experiences that reinforce what we perceive as reality.

Courageously Authentic will provide the tools, practices, and heartwarming stories of women like you who have embarked on a healing journey to reclaim their lives and reawaken as their true authentic selves.

I've had the honor to coach these women and share their journey as they rewrote their stories and took back their lives. I will also share my journey with you in the hope that you will no longer feel alone or misunderstood. May these stories, principles, and teachings touch your heart and give you the courage to begin your healing journey, loving yourself so deeply that you allow your true self to emerge and live as God intended you to.

The Day I Became Invisible

I was the youngest of three in my family—the "unplanned child," as my mother often reminded me. I was always invisible—an outcast. I never felt like I belonged . . . anywhere. I longed for the day when someone would value and accept me for my authentic self instead of measuring my worth by what I could do for them.

When I was five, I received an "Excellent" mark and a sticker on my paper from kindergarten. I couldn't wait to show my parents. "This will do it! They will be so proud of me," I thought. I pictured my paper behind a magnet on the refrigerator next to my sister's paper. I beamed as I ran through the front door and up the long hallway, stopping at the kitchen door. My mother stood at the stove, talking to her brother on the phone with her back to me. I couldn't wait for her to turn around so that I could share my big news.

Standing there waiting, I felt my heart might burst into a million pieces. I adored my mother. Like most children, I craved her attention and approval but rarely received it in the same way as my siblings. Then, in an instant, my heart stopped bursting. Instead, it shattered into those million pieces. "Brenda is such a burden sometimes," my mother explained to my uncle as she flipped the fried chicken. "She can be so difficult. She's not smart like the others. Sometimes, we wish she would never have been born."

She then turned and saw me standing in the doorway. She looked straight into my eyes, realizing I had heard everything she said. With the paper still clutched in my left hand, I watched my mother return to the stove and continue her conversation. I turned away and walked back down the long dark hallway as my paper floated slowly to the floor and tears streamed down my face. "What did I do to make Mommy hate me so much?" I thought to myself. "Why does Mommy think I'm not smart? I got an EXCELLENT and a sticker on my paper!"

That day, I became invisible. I stopped talking and spent most days by myself. I felt that way, I wouldn't be a burden to anyone.

That experience changed my life and led me to loneliness, despair, and low self-worth. Reflecting back on that day, I realize it was the moment I began my soul journey to becoming the woman I am today.

As the years went on, I became extremely introverted. I only talked when I had to. When I did speak, I was often criticized, made fun of what I said, or told I was wrong or stupid, even when I knew I was right.

In fifth grade, I was an above-average student. Yet, I was labeled as "slow" by my parents and the nuns at school simply because I refused to talk. The nuns' discipline toward me was excessive. They sent me to detention, threw chalkboard erasers at me, ridiculed me in class, and sent me to the principal's office numerous times. When I still wouldn't talk, I had to stand up in front of my classmates each week to attend a "special" class for children with learning disabilities. I didn't understand the reason for such humiliation, embarrassment, and mistreatment when my grades were actually above average.

Years later, I realized it wasn't about my grades or intellect. The nuns and my parents wanted to break my spirit and shame me so that I would conform to their control, belief systems, and conditioning. They were trying to pass on what they learned from their parents. They didn't realize that this form of discipline took my voice away and shattered my self-esteem and self-worth.

Without realizing it, I carried those belief patterns into my adulthood. I continued to attract similar relationships in both my personal and professional life—people I thought were friends but proved to be anything but. These people undermined me, betrayed me, lied to me, and took advantage of my loyalty, just as my siblings and family members had done. But this isn't where the story ends. As you continue reading, you'll learn how I stepped out of my shadow, removed the many invisible masks I hid behind for years, and reclaimed my life, just like the other women in this book.

I invite you to go on this journey with me, immersing yourself in the beautiful stories, challenges, and experiences of these women with whom I believe you'll identify. Through this self-discovery process, you will explore your shadow side, find your voice, rediscover your true authentic self, and take back your power. You'll learn why you experienced the trials, tribulations, and traumas in your life, the value of those lessons, and how the people in your past served as teachers in your "soul movie."

The information in these chapters is not an invitation for psychiatrists, psychologists, or different religious denominations to weigh in on your experiences and how you "should" have felt or to compare your experiences with survey data. Instead, you will turn to the expert who has firsthand knowledge of the emotional, spiritual, and physical impact your past had on your life. That expert is you.

Courageously Authentic will be your guide to self-discovery, self-love, and empowerment as you rewrite your story. So, are you ready to take that first step and be accountable for your healing? To remove the barriers, tackle shame, stop the old programming, and dare to love yourself and your inner child so genuinely that you believe you deserve the life you desire? It simply takes you saying, "Yes, I'm ready!" and having the dedication and commitment to begin your healing journey as you absorb the information contained within each chapter.

In addition to the stories and insights, you'll find simple yet powerful exercises that I've used and shared with others, resulting in remarkable transformations for both myself and those I've coached. You may complete some activities more quickly than others, but it's not about speed. It's about creating a safe space for self-discovery and

INTRODUCTION

compassion while honoring where you are in your healing journey. It's about self-reflection, forgiveness, and empowerment. It's about removing your invisible masks and reclaiming your life. It's about fearlessly showing the world your true authentic God-self and loving every part of you, regardless of others' opinions or outside influences. It's about being free.

Be gentle with yourself as you relate to these stories and work through the exercises. Love yourself for having the courage to heal. Treat yourself to a beautiful journal, a special pen, and a quiet place. Isn't it time to transform and take back your power? Let's do it together, Beautiful!

CHAPTER 1

WHAT'S HAPPENING TO ME?

"Behind every ego mask is a person who longs to be seen and understood." ~ Anonymous

As we embark on this journey together, my goal for writing this book and sharing women's stories is to give you the same support, knowledge, and principles I provided them and have used myself. I had the privilege to share their healing journey as they applied the lessons I'm sharing with you throughout these chapters. I watched these ladies emerge from their darkness into beautiful, powerful women who removed their invisible masks and revealed their authentic souls to the world as God created them perfectly.

The stories in this chapter will introduce four of the six women featured in the book. To start, you will get a glimpse of each woman's challenges. As you continue reading, you'll learn more about their journeys and how they applied the principles from these chapters to overcome their struggles.

These women faced significant challenges, including rejection, betrayal, and shame, which drove them to make radical changes. For years, however, fear prevented them from making these necessary adjustments. The misery, unhappiness, and low self-worth felt familiar, so they hung onto their old lives and secrets, not realizing their belief systems kept them paralyzed as victims. They remained trapped until the despair became so unbearable that they finally had the courage and determination to take steps to change their lives and reclaim what they lost—their purpose and themselves. Through these heartfelt stories, you'll witness the remarkable healing, self-discovery, and freedom they experienced.

May you find comfort and the courage to apply the same wisdom, principles, and exercises to your life. You deserve to be free. You deserve to be your true authentic self.

Shreya ~ Mirror, Mirror

I have always admired my friend, Shreya, for her strong, independent character. Kind and loyal, she has a grace and presence that leaves a footprint on your heart. Of Asian descent, she has beautiful, elegant features and long, reddish-brown hair.

While she was in Connecticut, the two of us met for lunch one day. We hadn't seen each other in a while, but we chatted through lunch as though no time had passed between us. Shreya wiped the crumbs off the tablecloth, folded her napkin, and placed it under her phone. That was a nervous habit she had, I remembered.

"Shreya, is there something bothering you?" I asked.

"I don't know how to say this. I'm ashamed to admit it, but I'm so unhappy. I don't know why. I have no reason to be unhappy. I'm in perfect health. I have a beautiful home, great kids, and a solid marriage. I love Reginald. He's a good husband. My job pays well, and I work with great people. But when I get up each morning, it takes every ounce of energy I have to put a smile on my face, start my routine, and pretend nothing's wrong," she told me as she sucked in a deep breath.

"Have you talked to anyone about this? A therapist? Does Reginald know how you feel?" I questioned.

"No. How would I explain my feelings? How could I tell him? I have everything a woman could possibly want, but I'm miserable and don't know why. I don't even understand what's going on with me. I have become so good at masking my feelings. I go through the day smiling, laughing, and performing my responsibilities, but I'm so exhausted that I can barely function by the end of the day. And then, I have to do it all over again."

She began to cry. I understood the kind of exhaustion and desperation Shreya spoke of, and I felt for her.

"The other day, I stood in the shower and cried until I couldn't cry anymore," she continued. "I don't know how long I can continue with this charade. I refuse to become my mother, Brenda."

Olivia ~ Alone in the World

Olivia and I were colleagues for several years. She was forty-six years old and wore her heart on her sleeve. She had strong integrity, worked hard, and cared deeply for people. With a kind heart and a soft voice, she chose her words carefully, especially when she shared feedback that could upset someone. She was the caretaker in her relationships and put the needs of others before her own. I suspect that's why she always looked disheveled. She wore a touch of blush on her pale cheeks and pulled her dirty blonde hair back into a sloppy bun.

The day she confided in me, her clothes were wrinkled, and her Mary Jane shoes were well-worn.

"My life is falling apart," she admitted, erupting like a volcano. "No matter how hard I try, I can't seem to break out of this cycle of bad luck. I feel like everyone's against me. This past year, my father died. The grief overwhelmed me so much that I gained fifty pounds. No one seemed to understand what I was going through. Everyone expected me to just return to my routine after a couple of months."

I'd never heard her say so much at once, so I just listened as she cried. But it took everything I had to maintain my composure as my stomach churned, and my own familiar grief returned. I knew her pain. I understood that kind of loss and the feeling that you were alone with no one who understood or cared to understand. The unspoken sorrow grips your heart so tight that you can't breathe. I took a deep breath and returned my focus to Olivia.

"My husband left me for another woman, and my kids blame me for the divorce. My friends no longer come around because I stopped doing everything for them like I used to do. I can't keep up. I'm just too tired to carry this heavy load," she continued. "I work in a toxic, tribal environment. My coworkers, who I thought were my friends, now ignore me. The culture is so politically corrupt that I feel pressured to compromise my integrity to fit in. People in the 'tribe' are held to different standards and not held accountable. Because I won't play the games, I'm now an outcast. I hate my job. I hate the culture. But where will I go at my age, Brenda? It seems like the more I pray and ask for help, the more bad things happen to me. I feel like I'm under spiritual attack. I've lost my faith. I don't know what to do or where to turn. I have no one." The look on her face showed her desperation, and my heart went out to her.

Julie ~ Impostor Syndrome

"Brenda, I'm handing in my resignation today," Julie said.
"I'm sorry to hear that. May I ask where you're going?" I asked.
"I don't know yet. I just know I can't stay here."
Julie was a tall, quiet woman in her late fifties.
"Are you comfortable sharing why you can't stay here?" I asked.
"It's not just this place; it's everything, Brenda."
I pointed to the chair, offering her a seat across from me. I placed my hands in my lap and sat quietly, waiting for her to speak. Julie sat down slowly, staring intensely at her hands as she nervously clasped them together.

"What's on your mind and so heavy in your heart? You don't have to worry about how to say it. Use whatever words feel comfortable for you. I'm not here to judge," I said.

"Brenda, I'm fifty-seven years old. This past year has been one of the most challenging years of my life, but it helped me realize I've spent my entire life living under the shadows of others. I lived my life by everyone's expectations and needs—what they wanted and expected of me. They never cared about what I wanted or needed."

"What people are you talking about?"

"Everyone in my life—my parents, relatives, siblings, and people I trusted as friends, lovers, bosses, and coworkers. I realized this past year that I've never had anyone who truly cared about me for me. I'm not a terrible person, Brenda!"

"I know you're not, Julie."

I listened as she reminisced about events in her life that still gripped her with pain.

"Why do I keep attracting these people into my life? All I've ever done is work. I never got to enjoy life. I put myself through undergraduate and graduate school with no support. I spent long hours at work and then at night school. I wouldn't get home until after 11:00 p.m. and back up by 4:30 a.m. I worked insane hours and carried a heavy course load at Northwestern University. On the weekends, I just needed an hour to clear my head and catch my breath, but my mother insisted I earn my keep. So, I spent hours on chores while my brothers and sisters did nothing. I finally moved out, and the morning I moved, my mother asked me for money to help pay the taxes. I told her I only had my saved coins, which was enough money to pay for next semester's books due that Friday. But she insisted I give her my coins, even though I knew she didn't need the money. That left me broke."

The shock on my face made Julie feel she needed to defend herself.

"I didn't have the energy to fight her, Brenda."

"I'm so sorry. I didn't mean to make you feel like you did something wrong or needed to explain why you gave your mom the money. It was the injustice of the situation that triggered me. I understand why you did it. I probably would've done the same thing. Sometimes, it just isn't worth the fight. Were you able to buy your textbooks for the semester?"

"Not before class started. I borrowed a classmate's books, but I had to wait until she finished studying to use them."

Julie took a long, deep breath and shook her head in surrender. "When I told my father that Stanford had accepted me in its MBA program, do you want to know what he said? He said, 'I don't know why you're wasting your time or money. You're not smart enough to make it through that program.'"

It pained me to hear how unsupported Julie had been. Her parents' lack of support set her up to be an adult with impostor syndrome.

"When I got engaged, I called my parents to tell them the exciting news. My mother couldn't even congratulate me. Instead, she shamed me for getting engaged before my brothers and sisters and berated me for the next twenty minutes. I told her she didn't have to come to my wedding and hung up. My father called me back, then my brother, then my sisters. Their words were so cruel and insensitive. No one was happy for me. I didn't talk to them for months after that, and I was too embarrassed to tell my fiancé the whole story."

Julie slumped in her chair, the emotional pain deepening on her face as she recalled years of memories. "I don't know why I'm sharing all this with you. It was so long ago. It's all in the past now. I can't change it," she said softly.

"You're right. You can't change the past," I told her. "But it's hard to heal when you continue to receive the same treatment from people you hope will care about you. A day comes when you're ready to change your life. Sometimes, this means walking away from everything and starting over. It's about taking back control of your life—taking back your power and to hell with the rest."

"Yes. That's why I need to leave. I feel miserable here. These people are so much like my family."

"Where will you go?"

"I don't know yet. I've got some money saved up. I'm going to take some time off. Travel. You probably think I'm crazy for quitting my job at my age."

"Not at all. What you're doing takes courage. I respect you for that. I hope you'll find the peace you're looking for."

"I don't know how to find peace. I sure haven't found it yet. Do you know how?"

"Well, in my experience, it's through forgiveness of both yourself and those who hurt you."

"How can I possibly forgive everything they did to me?" Julie asked, exasperated.

"You're not condoning what they did or forgiving their actions or treatment toward you. You're forgiving them so that you can set yourself free. I know this may be hard to understand now, but they were teachers in your life. You wouldn't be the strong, independent woman you are today, walking away from everything familiar to start a new journey if they didn't bring you to this point."

Julie winced as she stared at me for a long moment.

"Would you consider journaling about your experiences, memories, and feelings?" I pleaded.

"Why would I want to rehash all of those painful memories? I'm already miserable." Julie answered.

"Because those memories still control you, which is part of the reason you feel the way you feel. When we keep painful memories locked in our heart, the pain grows until we can't separate reality from illusion. It causes us to remain the unconscious victim, and the unhappiness can overwhelm us to the point where we question our worth, sanity, and purpose. Journaling can help you heal your heart and make sense of things, releasing years of anguish. It will help you find peace."

Julie agreed to consider my suggestion. She thanked me for listening and asked if she could reach out to me again. Of course, I said yes. But when she walked through the door, I wondered if I'd ever hear from her again.

Lizzie ~ The Hidden Secret

On a cold Sunday afternoon, I stopped by the local coffee house to pick up a hot caramel latté when I spotted Lizzie in a deep, seemingly contentious conversation with a man I assumed was her boyfriend. He stormed out, leaving Lizzie alone, looking upset and scared.

We had met at a fundraising event through work three years prior. We became instant friends—the type of friends who can just pick up where they left off regardless of how much time has gone by. I was surprised to see her in town since she lived in a condo thirty miles away from the coffee house and was attending school at Wesleyan University.

Lizzie was a beautiful, shy, kind-hearted woman from southern Mississippi, where her parents and three sisters still lived. Her sisters married young, had their own families, and worked at the church with their mother, while Lizzie was the only child in her family to go to college.

I was paying for my latté when she walked up to get a napkin. We greeted each other, and I asked how she was doing.

"I'm okay," she answered. "I'm just embarrassed everyone had to see that."

"Don't worry about it. Everyone is already back to their conversations." I said.

"Would you like to join me at my table? Do you have time?" Lizzie asked.

We sat down and talked about everything but the incident. I purposely didn't ask what happened. As distraught as she was, I wanted her to tell me in her own time. I could tell whatever transpired with that guy had rattled her to the bone.

An hour passed, and I needed to get to an appointment. Finally, I said, "Listen, I've got to run, but I just need to know you're safe before I go."

"It's nothing like that."

"Okay, good. Well, if you need anything, give me a call. Do you still have my cell number?"

"Yes, thank you, I do. I'll walk out with you." As she gathered her belongings, I noticed her hands were still shaking slightly.

A couple of weeks before Christmas, I received a call from Lizzie. She sounded desperate, and we agreed to meet again at the coffee house.

"I hope you don't mind me taking you up on your offer," Lizzie said when she arrived, "but I don't have anyone else I can talk to." This surprised me since I knew she was close to her sisters.

She explained that the guy she was arguing with was her boyfriend, and she had broken up with him. She became noticeably anxious.

"Lizzie, whatever you need to tell me is okay. I'm not going to judge you or share your information with anyone unless you tell me you're in physical danger. Then, we need to find you some protection," I said.

She took a deep, cleansing breath and sat back. "No, I'm not in physical danger. It's worse than that. I broke up with my boyfriend, Elijah, because I don't have the same feelings for him as he has for me. I thought he loved me enough that he would understand why, but he doesn't. He's from my hometown, and his family is close friends with my father. He's so mad at me for breaking up that he threatened to tell my father everything." The fear in her eyes was unmistakable.

"Tell your father what?" I asked softly.

Then, my dear friend burst into tears. "I'm so scared. My father will disown me. This information will hurt his position at the church and in town if it gets out. I should never have told my boyfriend the truth. I don't know why I told him."

* * *

The stories of these women reflect the internal struggles that so many of us live with daily—the feeling of wasting our lives away because we feel unworthy and remain stuck in others' belief systems and conditioning that we have accepted as our own. We hide behind our masks to stay invisible and play the role others expect from us. Our audience determines which invisible mask we choose to wear— the Victim, the Hero, the Perfectionist, the Pleaser, the Martyr, or any number of other masks.

Keep reading to learn more about their journeys, what they learned, and how they healed.

CHAPTER 2

BREAKING THE EGO'S SPELL: FREEING OUR BELIEFS FROM FEAR OF CHANGE

"In resisting change, we wage a silent battle against our true self." ~ Brenda Hukel

*A*re you ready to make a change in your life? I've asked this question thousands of times, and I'm never sure what response I'll get from those I coach. Some approach the change with excitement and anticipation. Some say they're ready but want a guarantee the change will go smoothly. Others display fear physically—a clenched jaw, a sudden uncomfortable movement in their chair, or eyes darting around the room. Others excuse themselves for a cigarette and never return, or they suddenly remember an appointment and leave abruptly.

Others express resistance to change emotionally—displaying signs of immediate victimism, reciting all the reasons why change doesn't work for them, or insisting it isn't the right time. Some start the blame game, suddenly becoming angry or stubborn. Some make excuses or try to manipulate the conversation. They interrupt, won't listen, and become combative or defensive. They try to intimidate and cause confusion in order to take control and create a distraction to take the attention off of themselves. Some do this by changing the subject to focus on someone who needs to change more than them. The list of avoidance strategies goes on and on.

Change is easier in our teens because we're looking for adventure. When we get older, we're looking for safety. However, when we resist change, we fight against ourselves. This creates needless suffering, frustration, and, ultimately, depression because we're stopping the natural flow of energy.

When we're in a state of resistance, we're out of alignment with our "True Selves." We're not operating in our authentic power but in a programmed state controlled by our ego.

There are many reasons people justify why they can't change. Some of the more common excuses are:

- I'm not the one who needs to change; they do! I'm the victim in this situation.
- My spouse would never understand or support me.
- No one can fix my problems. I'm too broken.
- Now is not the right time. I'll do it later.
- I'm too old to change now.
- I don't have the money.
- I don't have the energy. It'll take too long.
- Nothing will improve; why go through the effort?
- My changes will cause too much disruption and pain for my family and friends.
- I will lose my spouse, family, or friends. I'll end up alone.
- My parents would disown me if I made this change.
- It'll impact my status at work and in my community.
- My kids are too young. My focus needs to be on them, not me.

- I'll do it as soon as I … lose weight, get a new job, make more money, etc.

Why do we do this to ourselves? Why are we so afraid to explore an opportunity to make a change that will stop the endless cycle of pain, misery, illness, frustration, or fear in our lives? Because we're taught to believe change is hard and scary. We're told changing will cause more pain, failure, and uncertainty.

Instead of looking at the opportunity to heal and create positive outcomes to realign with our true authentic selves, we fall into the resistance mindset and become overwhelmed with the idea of changing. This is living in a third-dimensional consciousness, which is very dense and heavy energy. In this state, we operate in duality and separation. We examine our life and the world around us linearly. We function out of fear, lack, and judgment, creating separation. Our conscious awareness resists everything because if we can't use our five senses, our rational mind says it doesn't exist. While operating in this level of consciousness, our ego is in charge, and our mind overrules our heart. The tape playing in our head inhibits us from living authentically because to fit in, we believe we must conform to societal conditioning or those of our family, friends, culture, or religion. This vicious cycle creates anxiety and negative self-talk, justifying why we can't change. So we forget a very simple rule: *change your belief about change!*

Change Your Belief About Change

Our beliefs create our emotions, and our emotions determine our behaviors. We struggle with change because an underlying experience or an old wound causes an emotional trigger. The emotional trigger then rationalizes why the change is unwarranted. This is the voice of our ego, which doesn't want us to change. It wants to control us.

It controls us by keeping us in fear and resistance because the ego only thrives in the shadow of our unconsciousness. The ego's role is determined based on which of our wounds is triggered. This is when we select an invisible mask to hide behind and justify that authenticity is unsuitable or impossible for us. There are multiple ego masks we can hide behind—the Victim, the Martyr, the Perfectionist, the Villain, the Judge, the Pleaser, the Princess, etc.

When our mind is aligned with our ego rather than our higher consciousness, we operate from a negative belief system, which prevents us from following through with a change. In his book, *A New Earth: Awakening to Your Life Purpose,* Eckhart Tolle illustrates his theory regarding the impact of the ego and the significance of living in the present moment by explaining that the stronger the ego, the more control it has over us. In this state of being, it's impossible to live in the present moment because the ego lives on "time," not "timing." Therefore, our primary focus is on the past or future. The past represents our identity; the future represents the fulfillment of it. But the future is just that, the future—a world of problems, challenges, expectations, and disappointments because we're always waiting to accomplish the next thing before we believe we can find happiness. Of course, the only thing that exists is the present moment. We can't change the past, and the future never comes because it's always the future (Tolle 2005).

When we live in the present moment, we surrender our ego and the need to control the "time" of events and people. Instead, we trust God's "timing." This removes the polarization, definitions, and conditions placed on the outcome and allows changes to flow freely.

As we transition out of the old programming and into higher consciousness, we enter a "Limbo State," also known as the "Neutral State." This is a critical phase in which psychological realignments and re-patterning take place. In this state of awareness, we operate from our higher consciousness and trust God to orchestrate the next steps. We remain in the "NOW" and hold excitement without insistence or assumptions of a specific outcome, no matter what happens. When we stay positive and follow the path of least resistance, our higher mind (i.e., God) directs us. Through this transition of importance, our pure intentions and intent create our new reality in the present moment. The past and future are no longer relevant.

Imagine the freedom we would have if we didn't allow separation of consciousness, living under the illusion that we're powerless. We would lovingly allow God to move through our consciousness with grace and ease. We would trust that change is for our highest good.

In Shreya's case, the woman with a beautiful house, great kids, and happy marriage didn't want to interrupt that life. She feared telling her husband that she was unhappy. She didn't think he would understand and would call her ungrateful (even though she never complained). She feared it would break up her marriage.

When Shreya and I explored this belief about her husband, I suspected it was from a traumatic childhood experience. Her parents were wealthy and lived in an elite neighborhood. Her father was a successful attorney who was well-respected in their community. Her mother didn't work. Like most of the wives within that social circle, her mother took care of the family, hosted parties, attended charity events, and maintained a certain status.

Shreya attended the best schools and clubs and actively participated in sports, horseback riding, and dance classes. She was also the most popular girl in school.

She adored her parents but felt closer to her father. She loved spending time with him when she got the chance, but he worked long hours, traveled, and busied himself on the weekends with golf or stayed held up in his study with the door closed.

As I continued to ask questions about her childhood, Shreya became agitated. Her lips tightened, vertical wrinkles appeared between her eyebrows, and she clenched her jaw. As she glared at me, I said, "Talk to me about your mother."

"What does that have to do with anything?" Shreya asked defensively.

"Please, Shreya, answer my question," I said calmly.

"My mother and I don't talk much. She had it all. She was beautiful. She didn't have to work. We had maids, chefs, and groundskeepers. She shopped at the most expensive stores. She had lunch with her friends weekly and played tennis at the country club. My father gave her everything she wanted. I guess you could say she was spoiled."

"What happened between you and your mother that caused you to stop talking?" I asked.

"Mom was never happy. Around her friends or when she hosted parties, she acted like she was on top of the world—laughing, telling jokes, and even flirting a little. As soon as the guests were gone, she argued with my father and complained constantly. He worked hard, and nothing was good enough for her."

"What do you mean nothing was ever good enough for her?"

"What does this have to do with anything? I spent years forgetting about it!"

"Please indulge me for a little bit longer. I understand this is difficult."

Shreya let out a long sigh and rolled her eyes as she shifted in her seat. "My mom acted like she had the worst life possible. What more could she possibly want? My poor father worked all day, and as soon as he came home, she started in on him about how unhappy she was, how she wanted to spend more time with him, and he was never home."

"What did your father do in those situations?"

"He was patient at first. When Mom didn't stop nagging at him, he bought her a new car, sent her on a trip, or gave her whatever she wanted, but it was never enough."

Shreya leaned over, shoulders slumping. She crossed her legs and placed her hands under each thigh. Then, she uncrossed her legs and sat back hard against the chair.

I waited patiently for her to continue. She looked up, and I saw anger penetrate her eyes and spread across her face. I feared she would leave before discovering the emotional trigger that was causing her resistance to changing her situation.

"My mother had an affair, all right? Now you know. Are you happy? I let you in on the little family secret. She left my father for another man. It broke his heart. He was never the same after that. Everything changed. Everything!"

I knew her attempt to insult me was deliberate, and she intended to put me on the defensive so I would react, getting us off-topic. But I didn't go for it. Instead, I held eye contact with her and asked, "What do you mean everything changed? What changed?"

"My father drank every night until he passed out. He worked long into the evenings. He came home late, or he didn't come home at all. People talked. He stopped going to the club and interacting with his circle of friends. I guess you could say we lost our status," Shreya said with deep sadness and regret. "I never forgave my mom for breaking up our family. I'm still so angry at her."

"Shreya, thank you for sharing this with me. I know it was excruciating for you to talk about it, but it helps me understand your resistance and fear of making a change."

"I don't understand what my mother's selfish acts have to do with why I'm so miserable. I'm nothing like her!"

"Anger is often masked by unresolved grief. It's the sadness within us that had nowhere to go for a very long time. In your case, you never forgave your mother for being so unhappy that she chose another man and had an affair with him. Because your mother wanted happiness and companionship, she made a change that impacted both you and your father and disrupted your lives. She left your father, whom you adored. As a teenager, you didn't understand how your mother could be so unhappy when she had everything money could buy. Or how she could betray you and your father. You both lost your status and circle of friends. As you said, everything changed. Your mother wanted to share her life with someone who would pay attention to her and show her love, not shower her with material things. You formed a belief about your mother that she was selfish and broke up the family."

"I can't believe you're defending my mother!" Shreya shouted.

"I'm not defending her," I said calmly. "I'm simply peeling back the layers of your belief system so that you can see why you're so resistant to telling your husband how you feel. Your belief is you lost your father because your mother decided to leave, which caused your father to change. He drank more, worked longer hours, and left you home alone. This is unprocessed grief, and your grief is an emotional trigger. It's part of why you're afraid to tell your husband that you're unhappy."

"I don't understand."

I could see the emotional exhaustion starting to take a toll on Shreya.

"Your life mirrors your mother's, Shreya," I said softly. "You have a beautiful home, wonderful kids, nice car, many friends, and are active in the community. Money is plentiful. You and your husband are well-respected in your professions. Yet, like your mother, you feel miserable and are afraid to make a change to bring back the happiness you lost along the way. Unconsciously, you're afraid to tell your husband how you feel because you're worried it will turn out as it did with your mother. You don't want to be responsible for tearing apart your family or breaking the hearts of your children and husband—like you and your dad experienced."

I expected Shreya to react to my observation, but she sat motionless in her chair. So I continued.

"You feel angry at yourself because the one thing you never wanted to become was your mother. You have repeatedly said you never want to be like her, yet you do understand her pain."

"Oh, God!" Shreya gasped. Her eyes widened, and she covered her mouth with her right hand as her left hand instinctively went to her heart. I waited for her to comment. When she didn't, I kept going.

"You told me that you felt like you were losing your mind. You're not. You're simply lifting the veil to the unresolved pain and grief you never healed. This unleashed more anger toward your mother, but you're projecting your sorrow onto her. To avoid disrupting your family and facing more pain, you're willing to live with the misery, but it's reached a point where it can't be controlled or hidden as well as you've done in the past. Until you're willing to forgive your mother and yourself, you will struggle with changing your belief about healing this situation. A lack of forgiveness keeps you from moving forward. Forgiving your mother doesn't excuse what she did, but it can set you free."

Shreya looked at her hands. I remained quiet to let her process the information and possibly consider new beliefs. When she looked up, she nodded slowly.

Then, I asked my final question, "If there were no consequences for telling your husband how you feel, what would you tell him?"

Shreya's eyes welled up with tears, and she said, "I'm lonely. Just like my mother."

I nodded and repeated, "Just like your mother."

Her eyes opened wider. "Oh my God, Brenda! I never saw it before. I had no idea. I spent so many years hating her and holding onto so much anger. Now, I understand why she was so unhappy. Mom longed for what she and Dad had before they married, before the money, the status, and the responsibilities. She hid her pain and loneliness until she couldn't hide it anymore. Just like I'm doing." She paused. Why didn't Dad spend more time with her?"

"I don't know," I said. "That's a question for your father."

Shreya sat quietly. She looked exhausted.

"I know this is a lot of heavy, emotional information to process. You may need to take more time to sit with what we uncovered."

"I'm just amazed. Why didn't I see it myself?" she asked.

"It's difficult to see the truth when you're hurting. Sometimes the pain is so deep that it's easier to stay the victim and blame someone else so we can hold onto our story. This is when our ego keeps us in a negatively aligned belief system, so we remain in a state of fear."

Shreya nodded. "I'm going to talk to both of my parents."

"And your husband?" I asked.

"I'm going to talk to him first. I'm ready. I understand now. I'm so sorry I snapped at you, Brenda. Thank you for helping me see the truth."

Asking Shreya a series of questions enabled her to explore the beliefs that prevented her from talking to her husband, as well as identify the changes she needed to make.

What we fear the most about change is what we need to change the most. It's essential to understand our beliefs about resistance to change. We'll take an in-depth look at belief systems in the next chapter.

Shreya had spent years holding onto an old belief that her mother tore the family apart. On an unconscious level, her fear and anger masked her unhealed grief. Holding onto the anger toward her mother helped her justify why she couldn't forgive her mother for the pain she caused.

Shreya couldn't tell her husband she wasn't happy because she didn't know why she felt unhappy until we explored her beliefs about making a change. She believed that if she was honest with her husband, she would be responsible for tearing her family apart and couldn't bear the pain of going through that trauma again. When she thought about changing, it caused an emotional trigger, which she ignored until it consumed her so much that she felt she was losing control of her life.

In the following chapters, we'll explore the different levels of consciousness and how they create emotions and reactions as we ascend from third-dimensional reality to fourth-dimensional reality until we reach self-mastery—the fifth dimension.

Exercise: Making Changes in Your Life

This exercise will assist you in identifying areas you'd like to change in your life and the corresponding beliefs hindering your ability to change. We'll discuss this in more detail in Chapter 3, but for now, be as thorough as possible with your answers.

1. What's the first thing that comes to mind when you think about a change you want to make in your life? For example, end a toxic relationship, prioritize self-care, change jobs, get your degree, control spending, lose weight, etc.

2. Why do you want to make this change?

3. What beliefs about making this change keep you stuck? Unhappy? In fear? A victim? For example, if you're in a dysfunctional relationship, ask yourself what you have to believe about yourself to feel you deserve to be treated this way. What fear paralyzes you from making changes in your life that would bring you happiness? Why?

4. Where did this belief originate? Is it your belief or someone else's that you accept as your own? Can you recall how it was formed? Did it come from your parents, religion, or culture?

5. What excuse do you use to justify why you can't change or why the change won't work? Keep asking WHY questions until you've drilled down to the core issue.

6. What emotional trigger(s) do you experience when you think about making this change? Fear, anger, frustration, failure, anxiety, etc.?

7. How would you feel if you made this change?

8. What support do you need to make this change? It may be helpful to have an accountability partner during this process.

9. Pick one action you can commit to each week. Once you consistently integrate this action into your daily routine, celebrate your accomplishment, and continue to pick new actions one by one until you have mastered this change.

Write a simple yet powerful affirmation that you can recite several times a day to reinforce the success of this change. For example: "I release all beliefs preventing me from creating the life I desire and allow the change to manifest with ease and grace."

BREAKING THE EGO'S SPELL:
FREEING OUR BELIEFS FROM FEAR OF CHANGE

In reviewing your answers, what theme emerged? This discovery will uncover why you've struggled with making this change. To help identify your theme, look at your detailed explanations and circle the words you use repeatedly—for example: fear, control, anger, self-worth, shame, etc.

CHAPTER 3

WHO OWNS YOUR BELIEF SYSTEM?

"Breaking free from old beliefs is the key to unlocking your full potential to live the life you desire." ~ Brenda Hukel

I was sitting behind a closed door working on a highly confidential project when Olivia stormed into my office without knocking.

I looked up from my desk, shaking my head and thinking, "And so the day begins."

"Well, then, please come on in," I said to her. "I guess you didn't notice my door was closed? There was a reason for that."

"Oh, um . . . yeah, sorry. I need to talk to you. I want to file a complaint against my boss, Royce."

Exasperated, I said, "Olivia, what are you talking about? What type of complaint?"

"For being treated differently than my coworkers. Retaliation. Oh, and harassment, too."

"Sit down, please, and close the door. Again." I looked into her eyes, contemplating how I wanted to play this, and thought, "I'm going to call her bluff."

"What on earth is going on with you?" I asked her. "I've known you for over ten years, and this little performance is way out of character—even for you, Olivia."

"My boss is retaliating against me," Olivia repeatedly defiantly.

"How?" I asked.

"He's paying me back for taking unplanned time off to care for my brother. He's mad that he had to change his vacation because of my emergency, and now he took a huge project away from Gina and gave it to me. He's trying to set me up to fail. I have the heaviest workload in the department, and he said I have to fly to Colorado next week to meet with the clients." She exhaled a long breath before continuing with her rant.

"Do you have paperwork or something I need to fill out so I can file a complaint, or should I just get an attorney?" Olivia asked breathlessly.

I ran my hands through my hair and looked up at her.

"Olivia," I said stiffly. "Royce gave you that project because it's a game-changer for our company's success. He needs someone he can depend on with the knowledge and expertise to ensure the project is delivered on schedule and within budget. That's why he chose you. Didn't he tell you that he adjusted your workload and reassigned two of your large projects?"

"What's wrong with Gina?" she asked. "Why can't she finish it? He always liked her more than me. She always gets what she wants. We used to be friends until I stopped doing everything for her."

"Gina resigned last week when you were out on leave."

"Royce purposely scheduled the client meeting on Thursday so that you could have a long weekend in Colorado to visit your sisters. The company is paying for the added time to thank you for taking on the project. He met with me yesterday, and I approved it. Did he tell you he reassigned two of your projects so that you can focus on this one?"

"Well, he didn't have a chance," Olivia said as she lowered her head.

"Why?"

"When I heard I was getting another project, especially Gina's, I stormed out of his office and came straight here," she admitted sheepishly.

"I'm going to ask you one more time, Olivia. What's going on with you?"

She pressed her hands to her face, took a long, deep breath, began to cry, and said, "Oh, God. I'm so embarrassed. Royce has been so kind and understanding since my brother was diagnosed with advanced ALS. Since I transferred to his department, he really has been flexible with my schedule. I can't believe I lost it on him."

She shook her head and pinched the bridge of her nose. "I guess I brought my anger and frustration into work this morning. I got home late last night from my brother's. The kids left the house in a complete mess before leaving for their dad's. There were dirty dishes in the sink and on the table. The front room looked like the Tasmanian devil had stopped by for a visit. The clothes I washed and folded last night were all over the floor, and wet towels were on the bathroom floor. I was so hungry and exhausted. I felt so disrespected—it felt like they did it on purpose. You know they're still mad at me about the divorce, right? I don't know what their father tells them. He's the one who had an affair, not me."

"I would have been upset, too, but are you upset with the kids or yourself? The divorce was over eleven years ago. Are you sure the kids are still mad at you about it? They were babies at the time."

"I know how long my marriage has been over, Brenda! It doesn't make it any easier being a single mother. Please don't assume that it's my fault. He left us!"

"I'm not saying it's your fault, and I'm not saying it's easy to be a single mother. You're expecting different behaviors from your children, who aren't aware of your expectations. You've said so yourself that you don't discipline them or give them chores because you don't want them to hate you. Yet, you continue to come home to a messy house. There are never any consequences, boundaries, or rules for the kids. That's unhealthy. You do everything for them," I said gently.

Olivia sighed. "I don't want to lose them, too, Brenda. I already lost my husband to that bimbo."

"Teaching children responsibility, accountability, and respect are hallmarks of a strong, capable person. These are critical skills for anyone, regardless of age. You're angry because you feel your life has been unfair and controlled by external events," I said softly.

"It is. It has been!" Olivia said defensively.

"Hear me out for a second. You may not like what I'm about to say, but I'm asking you to set your ego aside because it just wants to prove me wrong and validate your beliefs about your life. Can you just hear me first?"

Olivia slumped back in the chair, folded her arms across her chest, and glared at me like a five-year-old whose lollipop was taken away for bad behavior.

"Okay," I said. "I'll take that as a yes. We all go through difficult times in our lives. When we continue to replay the same internal story in our head, it keeps us stuck as the victim. We remain the victim because we think our emotions and how we react validate the injustice done to us. But that isn't true. If external events controlled how we felt about a situation like a divorce, everyone who got divorced would feel the same way. They don't. Our beliefs about a situation affect our emotions and how we react. This is why so many people never heal from trauma because their beliefs are so ingrained within them that they struggle with moving forward. Instead, they hold onto negative emotions like bitterness, anger, victimism, and self-judgment. In their mind, this permits them to prove they're right and everyone else is wrong. Situations don't cause emotions; our beliefs about the situation do," I said.

"What are you saying?" Olivia asked.

"Your unhappiness is caused by your negative beliefs about your life. You're so adamant about being right and staying the victim, especially about your divorce, that you've alienated everyone who challenges your opinion."

I paused to gauge her reaction. I knew this was hard feedback to receive, but it was also essential for her to hear. "Until you're able to change your beliefs and be open to other opinions that provide different perspectives, you'll continue to struggle," I explained.

"I don't need to hear anyone's opinion. I'm right," Olivia snapped.

"Are you?" I challenged.

She continued to glare at me. I wasn't sure if she was absorbing the richness of the conversation and my knowledge on the topic or if she wanted to reach over and slap me. My guess was the latter.

"Olivia, our need to be right begins during our childhood. Do you know why?" I asked her.

"Why?" Olivia said in an over-exasperated tone, not missing the opportunity to roll her eyes.

"What do you do when your kids receive an A+ on a test?"

"Like any mother, I make a big deal out of it and reward them. Sometimes, I make cookies, or we go out for ice cream. Every A+ gets an extra $5 in their allowance," Olivia said proudly.

"How do your kids feel when they get an A+ vs. an F?"

"That's a stupid question. How do you think they feel?"

"Just answer the question, please."

"They feel smart. They're happy. They want everyone to know. They're the center of attention."

"Exactly. When a child gets an A+ on a test, they correlate the happy emotion they feel with being right. Because they answered all the questions correctly, they're rewarded and receive validation for being smart. When we're older, our feelings are associated with being right to recreate the happy emotions and validation we felt as kids. So when someone's opinion contradicts our beliefs about a situation, especially an emotionally charged situation like a divorce, it threatens our ability to recreate that happy emotion. This activates our feelings of shame, unworthiness, and the fear of looking foolish or being wrong. It drives our need to prove to everyone that we're right and they're wrong. This is a missed opportunity to change and release old programming that's keeping us stuck."

Olivia's face flushed. Her neck turned bright red, and her jaw tightened. I could tell she wanted to leave, so I continued before she got up.

"Olivia, I know this is difficult feedback to hear, but I'm asking you to spend some time exploring your beliefs about the divorce, your life, and why you continue to feel the need to hold onto the "judge and victim" mentality. It would be helpful for you to uncover where your beliefs originated so that you can heal. Will you do that?" I pleaded.

Olivia abruptly rose to her feet. I saw the anger flare in her eyes as she snapped her head around to face me. "I thought if anyone understood, it would be you, Brenda. I never expected you would take his side. I can barely keep up with my schedule, and now you expect me, who didn't break up my marriage, to spend time examining why I'm at fault."

"Again, I'm not taking anyone's side, and I'm not saying you're at fault. I'm simply asking you to remove your emotions and the need to be right so that you can look at your life objectively. Like all of us, you have a program running in your consciousness that feeds your negatively aligned belief system about your life. Until you examine that belief system and where it originated, your ego will continue to create resistance and maintain control over you."

I stood, our eyes locked, and with gentle compassion, I said, "Olivia, you're the only one who can change your life, but your desire to change has to be stronger than your need to remain the victim."

She turned and stormed out of my office without saying another word, slamming the door behind her. I shook my head and said a silent prayer for her.

The Power of Belief Systems

You can find various documentaries and research on how belief systems are defined and at what age they start. According to Oxford English Dictionary (OED)[1], a belief system is defined as: "Belief in or acknowledgment of some superhuman power or powers (esp. a god or gods) which is typically manifested in obedience, reverence, and worship; such a belief as part of a system defining a code of living, esp."

Collins Dictionary[2] defines belief system as, "The belief system of a person or society is the set of beliefs that they have about what is right and wrong and what is true and false."

The purpose of dedicating an entire chapter to belief systems is to demonstrate their powerful impact on our lives and overall well-being (both positive and destructive). Without going too deeply into the philosophical, scientific, or medical viewpoints on this topic, I will explore some of the research demonstrating how our belief systems control our lives.

Studies differ on what age children form their belief systems. Some psychologists theorize that behavior patterns start at age seven, while other studies show it as early as age four.

According to a study in the *Indian Journal of Psychiatry*, a child's capacity for forming belief judgments begins at the age of five (Rao et al. 2009). As adults, we base our lives on the information we absorb during childhood, which is shaped by learned experiences. From these experiences, we develop beliefs and judgments, storing them as memories. The information stored in the brain becomes intertwined with our conscious and unconscious emotions. The researchers further imply that the entanglement of these beliefs and emotions might be why people

---

[1] Oxford English Dictionary. 2nd ed. (Oxford: Oxford University Press), s.v. "Belief System."

[2] Collins Dictionary. (HarperCollins Publishers), s.v. "Belief System." Retrieved from: https://www.collinsdictionary.com/us/dictionary/english/belief-system.

feel threatened or react with unwarranted aggression when they perceive their beliefs to be challenged.

However, as children, our beliefs were predicated on our parents' opinions, emotions, values, and rules. Our parents' beliefs, perceptions, and judgments reflected how they felt about themselves, which existed before we were born. They defined what was right, wrong, bad, or good, which consistently played out in every conversation we overheard or were part of, which formed our reality. At this young age, we're operating from our subconscious mind because our conscious mind isn't developed yet. So we don't possess the ability to form our own opinion. We operate solely from emotions. We agree with our parents to gain their approval. Then, other people, society, religion, and culture, to name a few, also influence our beliefs.

Our subconscious mind replays our unhealed beliefs, determining our thoughts and feelings, which affect our behavior and decisions. We can change our beliefs at any time because it's a choice. However, it isn't as easy as simply choosing a different belief. Depending on the intensity of our emotional response and how deeply ingrained these beliefs are within us, they can distort our perception of reality. The more impactful the emotional experience, the higher the probability of perceiving the belief as true when it isn't.

Take those who suffer from anorexia nervosa disorder. They believe they're overweight. Their emotions supporting this belief are so strong that it drives their decision not to eat as they over-exercise and hide their condition. An anorexic may weigh eighty pounds, but when she looks in the mirror, she believes she is severely overweight. Charged by her emotions, she takes drastic measures to lose more weight.

A belief formed at a young age can stay with us for life if we possess no awareness of where it originated and fail to change it to improve the quality of our life. For example, in the story I told in the *Introduction,* I overheard my mother telling my uncle that I wasn't as smart as my siblings and was a burden to her. She wished I'd never been born. Hearing such hurtful messages at a tender age from a woman I adored and craved approval from shattered my heart and encoded a belief in my mind that I was unworthy and unlovable. I carried this belief into adulthood, attracting people and experiences aligned with those beliefs. It wasn't until I understood how beliefs work and the impact on the subconscious mind, body, and decision-making process that I realized I couldn't heal that experience until I chose different beliefs to heal the effects of that trauma.

When a core belief resides in our subconscious mind, it can cause an emotional trigger and reaction to a situation, and we may not know why we responded the way we did. Until we identify the core belief driving our emotions and where they originated, we'll continue to struggle with making or sustaining changes in our life, thus remaining the victim (consciously or unconsciously).

Being a victim is a learned behavior. As children, we watch adults play the victim role, creating scenarios to get their way or manipulate others to diminish the impact of their actions when they deliberately or unintentionally make a mistake. Some become masters of manipulation, creating scenarios and using others to blame so they can remain the wounded victim. It gives a false sense of power and control and excuses them, in their mind, from taking accountability for their actions.

Daniel, a deacon who served as a spiritual advisor to parishioners, was married to a beautiful woman with a job that required her to be actively involved in the community. She was well-respected and adored, but Daniel was jealous of his wife's many admirers and her deep devotion and dedication to her role in the community. His jealousy became so intense that it caused issues with their marriage. He would accuse her of adultery, become enraged over the time she spent helping others, and disparage her for not giving him the same amount of attention.

Father Paul, the priest of the congregation, started hearing whispers of Daniel's relationships with other women in the parish, with whom he spent time providing spiritual guidance. It became apparent that he was manipulating these women by creating a codependent relationship with them. They were lonely, vulnerable, and hungry to feel worthy of someone's attention. When Father Paul brought up his concerns, Daniel became defensive and argumentative. As the conversation heated up, Daniel blamed his wife for his own behavior, accusing her of infidelity. Father Paul had known Caroline for many years and didn't believe Daniel's accusations, but he could see that Daniel's behavior was causing the demise of their sacred contract of marriage.

So Father Paul invited Daniel to spend the afternoon with him, as well as time in prayer. Daniel shared that when he was in high school, he learned of his father's indiscretions with other women. His friends teased him mercilessly. This scarred Daniel deeply. He was angry at his mother for not leaving his father, and he hated his father for the embarrassment and shame he caused the family.

As Father Paul listened, he recognized that Daniel's fear of losing his wife and his strong need to have full control over her originated from his experiences as a teen. But Father Paul didn't feel Daniel had the awareness to see that his actions of manipulating vulnerable parishioners and emotionally abusing their goodwill was the same behavior as his father's.

Father Paul shared his observations and reminded Daniel that we're here to stay in God's grace through forgiveness, but Daniel immediately defended his actions by continuing to blame his wife. Unconsciously, Daniel was justifying his behavior because he never healed his own trauma. Instead, he became bitter, hid behind his collar, and inflicted pain on other women and his wife because he chose to remain the victim. He chose not to heal.

When you heal, you're accountable for your beliefs, emotions, and changing your behavior. This removes the victim mentality. Unfortunately, Daniel didn't begin his healing journey until many years after he lost his wife and his position in the church.

Your belief system controls what you consider truth and reality. The stronger the emotion, the higher the probability of dismissing others' opinions, even if they have facts to prove your incorrect interpretation. As a result, you might become adamant about proving you're right and others are wrong. Emotionally, this creates an internal struggle because you're operating from a belief system that isn't congruent with reality. So you resist changing your belief system because the realization of the illusion creates fear. This lack of awareness will divert your attention to the need to change others' beliefs and continue to find people who agree with your interpretation, even when you're wrong. This creates a lot of wasted energy, distractions, and emotional distress. And because your ego dictates your need to be right, you'll avoid alternative beliefs regarding the situation. It's a vicious cycle that will repeat until you identify the internal wound that needs healing.

I've seen this paradigm with successful executives, business owners, college students, and high-potential employees. When they're provided feedback that needs improvement, their ego immediately engages, and they're unable to hear the value of the feedback. Instead, they dismiss it because their belief system and internal emotional chatter don't align with their interpretation of the truth. They seek out people who reinforce their story so that they can remain the victim and prove the others wrong.

How often have you rehearsed a conversation in your head after someone upset you? Maybe you rehearse it in the car, when you're out for a walk, in the shower, or working out. That way, you will be ready to prove you're right and they're wrong. Your mind participates in the game and plays the other person while supplying you with their response to your attack. You select your words carefully because you intend to get your point across. Regardless of what the person said, it has no power unless their belief challenges yours. When you do this, your emotions get so tangled up with the need to be right, activating your ego to report front and center, that you don't realize what's going on—you're experiencing an emotional trigger.

An emotional trigger is a byproduct of your belief system that resides in your subconscious. If you can remove the emotions and look at the situation objectively versus the need to attack or react, you'll realize it's a mirror to unhealed trauma. Identify the belief and where it originated from, and you'll understand that the person who upset you is serving as a teacher to bring your awareness to what needs healing. It isn't about them; it's about you releasing your ego and healing the trauma. It's a mirror of how you're treating yourself. Heal your beliefs, and you'll no longer experience the emotional trigger.

Healing your belief system is vital to having a healthy life. As discussed in Chapter 2, how many times have you tried to make a change and failed? You become frustrated and can't stick with the required discipline. What happens, then? Your mind begins the negative self-dialogue, tearing down your self-esteem and self-worth, engaging in self-judgment. Then, your emotions spiral out of control. When this happens repeatedly, you form new beliefs—new facts ingrained in your subconscious because of your experiences. You likely take it a step further and compare yourself to people who, unlike you, accomplished the goal you set out for yourself. This thinking causes you to become a hostage to the emotional stories that feed your mind.

Out of desperation, you may resort to journaling, manifestation techniques, visualization, meditation, reciting affirmations, or other modalities, hoping for that little gem of happiness. When that doesn't work, you might spiral even further and become more discouraged, only to be disappointed again.

Do you wonder why this keeps happening? Why do you continue to struggle after all the time, effort, and money you've spent to make changes? The answer to these questions is simple: you haven't changed your core beliefs about what you're trying to change. Your beliefs about the change drive your emotions, which determine your behavior. This activates the negative mind, creating resistance and controlling what you communicate to yourself and others. And your subconscious mind can't discern between beliefs and facts. It stores beliefs in your memory as facts.

Beliefs play a significant role in shaping our perception of reality. They can either ignite our inspiration and drive us toward success or constrain our progress, potentially resulting in failure. This accounts for the differences in which people tackle demanding circumstances and explains why some flourish while others stumble.

Sometimes, it's easier to examine your feelings, which can then help you identify your belief patterns. You can do this by paying attention to the words you think and say throughout the day. If someone followed you with a recorder and played back your dialogues at the end of the day, what would you hear? Do you find the good in situations? Are you positive? Complimentary? Happy? Do you display humility and compassion? Do you engage in conflict without becoming defensive? Or are you negative? Do you complain? Do you gossip? Do you blame others? Do you become combative when given constructive feedback? Do you present yourself as the victim or brag about yourself to others? Do you put others down? Are you constantly apologizing for things you don't need to apologize for?

What thoughts are playing out in your head? *I hate this job. I can't stand her. My boss is an idiot who isn't qualified; it should be me. Nobody appreciates me. Why do I always have to work so hard? Everything is a constant struggle. I hate my body. I can never lose weight because diets don't work for me. I'm always sick. I never feel good. I'm so stupid.* Or do you focus on positive thoughts? *What a beautiful day. I'm so grateful for my job. I love my friends. I live in a beautiful home. I feel blessed to have a wonderful husband and loving children. I have people in my life who love me. I'm grateful for my health. I'm fortunate to have money in the bank.*

Changing your beliefs about a situation will change the outcome because as your thoughts and words change, they create different emotions and experiences. Negative vs. positive experiences depend on you.

Repetition is essential if you want to change your life to experience more positive outcomes. This requires you to keep your energy, beliefs, and emotions at the highest vibrational level. This is when the affirmations, manifestation techniques, and other modalities work because you're consistent with the practice and believe you will receive what you desire.

Let's take a look at Olivia and the impact of her childhood belief system. When she came to me, she felt despair and anger. She was at the end of her rope. She felt spiritually, physically, and emotionally exhausted and wanted me to support her belief about her life. After years of overextending herself for everyone else's needs, she finally reached a breaking point. She hid behind many ego masks as a survival mechanism until she lost her identity—who she was at her core. Because of her childhood experiences, she was conditioned to believe that her worth depended on serving others to the detriment of her own well-being. Only then, she believed, would she receive validation, love, and acceptance from others.

Once Olivia started exploring her core beliefs, thoughts, and the words she spoke throughout the day, she realized how her belief patterns had controlled her life and kept her stuck as a victim. Through this awareness, she dug deeper into where her belief patterns originated—her childhood.

Olivia's Childhood Trauma

Olivia grew up as the eldest of six children, and she turned ten the day her mother was diagnosed with stage four ovarian cancer. She remembers coming down the stairs, excited to celebrate her birthday. She couldn't wait to open her presents and eat cake and ice cream until her stomach hurt. She loved birthday cake—vanilla with chocolate icing was her favorite. She knew she would finally get that pink bicycle with the white seat and matching basket. The previous year, she saw it in a store window and saved her money, but she was still short $53 the last time she counted.

"I'm just bound to get my bike. I've been good for almost a month," Olivia thought as she bounced down the stairs in her favorite floral dress and white frilly lace socks with pink embroidered flowers.

But she stopped when she overheard her parents talking. "Why is Mommy crying?" she thought.

She knew it was wrong to eavesdrop and didn't want to lose another week's allowance, but she wanted to know who had upset her mother.

She quietly lowered herself to the stair, praying it wouldn't creak, and leaned her head between the wooden railings in order to hear her parents' voices. Remembering how much trouble she got into for eavesdropping before, she looked up at the number of stairs she would have to quickly run up to escape to her bedroom if her father got up from the table.

"What are we going to do, Jack? How are we going to tell the children?" she overheard her mother say.

"We'll fight it. We'll get you the best treatment there is," her father said with desperation in his voice.

"You heard the doctor. It's stage four. Even if we could get the best treatment available, where would we get the money?"

"Please don't talk like that. We can..."

"Stop. Please. My babies. My sweet babies. We need to make arrangements. We need to tell our families."

Olivia felt confused. "What was Mommy talking about? Stage four? What do they need to tell the family? Is she having another baby? I hope it's a girl. The last thing I need is another brother," she thought.

Her father scooted back in his chair and stood. Not wanting to get caught, Olivia shot up the stairs taking two at a time, darting back into her bedroom. She lay on her bed, her heart pounding, hoping her father hadn't heard her. She lay still, not moving a muscle so that she could hear if her dad come up the stairs.

She wasn't sure how much time passed before her father opened her bedroom door and turned on the light. She rubbed her eyes, realizing she had fallen asleep. "Is the birthday girl ready for her present?" her father asked.

"Oh, yes, Daddy! Did I get my bike? Did I, Daddy?" she exclaimed.

"You'll have to see. Everyone is downstairs waiting for you. How about a piggyback ride for the birthday girl?"

Olivia jumped up, swung her arms around her father's neck, and giggled.

"Oh, Daddy, I'm so excited. I can't wait to open my presents. I'm nearly a teenager."

He ignored that statement and bounced down the stairs, making horse sounds and bucking his body like he would buck her off. She squealed with delight, followed by deep belly laughs as she tightened her grip.

"There's my beautiful birthday girl," her mother said as Olivia reached for her and wrapped her arms tightly around her neck.

"I love you, Mommy."

"I love you, too, sweet girl. Now, how about you blow out these candles and make a wish!"

Everyone ate cake and ice cream. Olivia opened her presents from her brothers and sisters, hiding her disappointment that she didn't see her bike. When she heard a bell, she turned to see her dad pushing the same bike she had seen in the store window. It had a big red bow on the handlebars. It had a banana seat with an explosion of colored daisies. The white basket adorned a pink flower centered in the middle. Her eyes widened, and her cheeks turned red with excitement.

"For me? Is it really for me? I've waited so long." And then, through her excitement, she cried. She wiped her eyes with her arm through sobs and hiccups and thanked her parents. "Now, I can ride with my friends to the clubhouse and be part of the secret club. Thank you, Mommy. Thank you, Daddy. I'm so happy!"

Olivia jumped on her bike. Her mother looked so happy, but then, her eyes filled with tears.

Years later, sitting in my office, Olivia realized that her mother was probably grief-stricken that it would be the last birthday she would share with her eldest daughter. She imagined her mom slipping into the kitchen and burying her face into a kitchen towel as she sobbed quietly.

As a child, Olivia forgot about the conversation she overheard between her parents. She enjoyed the short summer and loved being the envy of her friends with her new bicycle. Then, one hot August day, she walked through the front door, letting the screen door slam behind her. Hungry, hot, and thirsty, she got a tall glass of lemonade from the refrigerator and sneaked a cookie before dinner when she saw her parents sitting at the kitchen table. Her mother was crying, as her father cradled her hands.

"Mommy, what's wrong?" Olivia asked.

"Olivia, your father and I need to talk to you. Please sit down."

"Did I do something wrong, Mommy?"

"No, no, not at all."

"Olivia, Mommy is very sick," her father said. "Mommy has a bad disease that is incurable. It's called cancer." He struggled to keep his voice steady.

"Can't you take her to the doctor and have him fix her, Daddy?"

"No, we already asked the doctor." Her father reached across the table to take Olivia's hand.

Her heart started to beat faster, and sweat ran down her back. She was petrified as she waited for her father to continue.

"We'll need your help around the house more. Mommy won't be able to keep up, and I have to work. We'll need you to help care of your brothers and sisters and pick up more chores around the house. Whatever Mommy needs. Can you do that? Can you be Mommy's little helper?"

As the weeks went on, Olivia managed the household—cooking, cleaning, bathing her younger siblings, and reading to them as she tucked them in for the night. Her father got home late from work, ate, and sat by her mother's bed. Olivia wouldn't go into her mother's room. She was told not to disturb her because she needed her rest.

As a result, Olivia felt alone and isolated, as well as angry that she couldn't play with her friends. She loved when her grandmother visited because she had someone to help her, but her grandma only stayed for a week because she lived too far away.

As the days passed, Olivia became more impatient, frustrated, and angry at her mother for being sick. She resented having to shoulder so much responsibility, and she wondered how long she would have to carry such a heavy load.

One afternoon, she felt so frustrated with her brothers that she thought she would explode. They wrestled in the front room, arguing over a toy, and she yelled at them to stop. She took the toy away and sent them outside to play. Ten minutes later, after she straightened up the front room, she looked out the bay window to check on her brothers playing tag in the front yard. She saw her friends ride by on their bicycles and felt a pang of jealousy. The anger welled up inside her until she thought, "That's it. I'll march into Mommy's bedroom and tell her how unfair it is. I don't care that I'm not supposed to bother her."

Olivia approached her mother's door. Her heart pounded as she clamped a sweaty hand around the cold door handle. Defiantly, she swung the door open. Before she could say anything, the image of the woman lying in her mom's bed took her breath away. She didn't look like her mother at all.

Her mother passed away that evening. As Olivia lay in her own bed, she was overwhelmed by feelings of grief, guilt, and despair. How could she have been so selfish? "I'm such a bad girl. Mommy will never forgive me," she thought.

Olivia never recovered fully from her mother's death. Her father remarried the following year, and even though her stepmother was somewhat of a surrogate mother, she couldn't replace her own mother's love, grace, and gentleness. So she never bonded with her stepmother. In fact, none of the kids did. They continued to depend on Olivia, and she felt a strong responsibility to devote her life to caring for her siblings.

She was surprised to uncover two unconscious core beliefs that she had formed after losing her mother to cancer. She believed she didn't deserve happiness because she felt that her deep-rooted anger was responsible for her mother's death. The second core belief was that in order to feel worthy, loved, and validated, she had to take care of the needs of others before her own. She vowed never to show her frustration like she felt toward her mother when she was sick. Subconsciously, she believed this diligent devotion would prevent her from feeling more guilt and sorrow. She wouldn't be the reason for anyone else's death.

Olivia's story demonstrates the powerful impact of beliefs and how they can control the quality of our lives. What beliefs about yourself keep you stuck? Unhappy? In suffering? The need for control? The need to be right and prove others wrong? What childhood beliefs are you holding onto that aren't yours? Which ego mask are you wearing? The Villain, the Victim, the Judge, the Pleaser, the Martyr, the Princess, or others?

Did you grow up hearing things like:

"As long as you live under my roof, you will do as you're told and keep your mouth shut!"

"I didn't ask you for your opinion. Your opinion doesn't matter."

"You'll never be successful. Your job is in the home."

"Children are seen, not heard."

"Your needs aren't important. Your job is to take care of your family."

"You will eat what's on your plate and like it, or go to bed hungry."

Or did you grow up in a family that believed in you? That told you that you were a powerful, strong, independent girl who could move mountains? That you're unstoppable and can achieve whatever you want? That you're talented, smart, and funny? That if you just believe, you can enjoy a life filled with happiness and success?

Can you feel the change in energy between the heavy, dense, negative conditioning vs. the confident, encouraging, and positive frequency that raises your vibrational energy and thoughts? Remember, others' beliefs about you hold no power over you unless you give them power.

As you've learned in this chapter, your belief systems are powerful mechanisms and can substantially affect how you live your life, what you think, and how you feel. Today is yesterday's tomorrow. Everything you experience is playing out from yesterday because of your belief system.

It takes twenty-one days to initiate a change in pattern. By choosing different beliefs, you can redefine your reality, watch your life change, and emerge into the person you desire to be.

A Special Message

To all the women and men who serve as role models to children, ask yourself what beliefs you're passing on to them. Are you passing on the beliefs you were conditioned to believe about yourself? Beliefs that allow you to control them through shame, power, or manipulation? Or are you passing on beliefs that inspire your children to have the courage, confidence, and perseverance to manifest the life they desire, even if it contradicts what you want for them?

Our children are the future leaders in this big, complicated world. Let's teach them to know and claim their power! To develop healthy, happy belief patterns that belong to them, not us. Let's enable them to believe they can succeed. Let's teach our children to believe in themselves and have humility, accountability, and respect. To be limitless. Let's teach them to be authentic. Let's be role models to our future leaders and generations. Let them grow into the unique beings God created and give them the wings to fly.

Exercise: Exploring Your Belief System

In the previous chapter, you identified a change you wanted to make and the limiting beliefs preventing you from making that change. This exercise will guide you deeper into your belief system and help you release outdated thoughts so that you can create new experiences.

Below are suggestions to guide you through this exercise.

1. **Identify your Core Beliefs**: It's essential to distinguish between what YOU believe, not what others impose upon you or expect of you. The more honest you are with your answers, the faster the healing begins. When you uncover a belief or peel back a layer of beliefs, sit with that information, and gently process your emotions by writing in your journal. There are no wrong answers. You feel what you feel. Remember, it's not

about judgment; it's about getting to the core of your belief system and allowing healing to occur.

2. **Embrace your Emotions**: You may be surprised by the emotions you experience when you discover where some of your deep-rooted belief(s) originated and from whom. That's okay, but you'll also want to release the blame, hate, anger, or resentment toward the person who influenced the beliefs. When you hold onto these toxic emotions, it only hurts you, not them, because adults repeat the beliefs instilled within them without understanding the damage they inflicted. It's a learned behavior. This isn't to excuse their behavior but to encourage you to forgive them so that you can free yourself.

3. **Engage in Self-Love and Compassion**: Refrain from judging yourself. Instead, be gentle, as if you're helping a five-year-old understand why she's hurting. That five-year-old is your inner child who wants to be healed and loved.

4. **Take Frequent Breaks**: Take your time. This exercise isn't intended to be completed in one sitting. Remember that you're allowing yourself to feel emotions you may have hidden for years. Take a break if you need it. Walk in nature, take an Epsom salt bath, do a workout, or engage in whatever activity will help you release the energy.

We hold many beliefs that prevent us from living our desired lives. What we believe and the energy we invest in our thoughts become our reality and shape our future experiences. However, beliefs can be changed, and now that you understand their power, your past no longer needs to define you. Your issues no longer need to be your truth. Change happens in the present moment, and by changing your beliefs, you transform your life. Let's begin.

1. What belief(s) keep you paralyzed, stuck, or have negatively influenced your life?

2. How have these beliefs limited you?

3. Where did these beliefs originate, and from whom? Were they passed down from generation to generation?

4. Is this belief still true for you? Why or why not?

5. Do you recognize that your limiting beliefs weren't based on your reality but on that of others?

6. How would your life be different if you didn't have these toxic beliefs?

7. As difficult as it was, what lesson did you gain from this experience? What did the beliefs teach you? For example, has it given you the courage to take back your power, make you stronger and more independent, say no, or are you ready to walk away from disrespectful, overpowering people, etc.?

8. Are you willing to replace your negative beliefs with new, empowering beliefs that reflect your true, beautiful self?

9. Review your list of old, outdated beliefs, and replace them with new positive beliefs. As you write your new belief statements, try to start each with I AM. Beginning an affirmation with I AM directs the energy straight to you and holds more power. It's a declaration to the universe that you know you deserve and are ready to receive these blessings. It realigns your negative ego mind as positive energy flows through your heart, and your intentions are released into the universe for manifestation. For example, I AM grateful for what this experience taught me. I AM worthy. I AM successful. I AM

deserving of the life I desire. I AM beautiful. I AM awakened to my new life, and everything flows effortlessly.

10. After you've completed your I AM statements, prioritize them and pick the top two or three. Close your eyes, take three deep breaths, and relax. Recite the first statement out loud. Feel the emotions it evokes. How does it feel to manifest your I AM intention? What does it look like? What colors and images do you see? Write your reflections in your journal.

11. Once you've mastered that feeling, try another statement. If you can only focus on one, that's fine.

12. Recite your affirmation several times a day. It's essential that you believe what you're stating is manifesting. This requires patience.

To help you remember, make your affirmation your wallpaper on your phone, put it on stickies around the house, your mirror, or in your car—whatever works best for you. Continue this practice, and watch the positive changes start to unfold.

CHAPTER 4

UNMASKING IMPOSTOR SYNDROME

"The true obstacles lie not in who you perceive yourself to be, but in who you overlook the chance to become." ~ Author Unknown

FEAR. A one-syllable word that can drive us to make positive changes in our lives or destroy us as we continue to live behind emotional masks and stay hidden from the world. And all because we're too afraid to live as our true authentic selves.

We believe that these invisible masks protect us from our vulnerabilities and allow us to hide our weaknesses and insecurities, but they don't. They create an illusion and false reality that contradicts our genuine authenticity.

Impostor Syndrome affects people across the globe regardless of fame, social status, wealth, or age. It's a paralyzing fear of being found to be not good enough or a fraud. How long can we play this charade? Until we decide to heal.

Impostor syndrome, also referred to as fraud syndrome, can occur in anyone at any time, whether a college student or a successful executive running a billion-dollar company. According to an article titled, "The Impostor Phenomenon," published in the *International Journal of Behavioral Science*, research shows that an estimated 70 percent of people experience these feelings at some point in their lives (Sakulku 2011); more recent studies show as high as 82 percent (Bravata et al. 2020).

The psychological term, "The Impostor Phenomenon," was coined by psychologists Dr. Pauline Clance and Suzanne Imes in 1978. In an article published by Clance and Imes (1978) called "The Impostor Phenomenon in High Achieving Women: Dynamics and Therapeutic Intervention," they discuss their research findings of more than 150 women who believed they were intellectual frauds. They feared being found out as impostors. Impostor phenomenon refers to the experience in which individuals doubt their own achievements and fear being exposed as fraudulent, despite evidence of their competence and achievements.

These women were highly successful individuals who possessed advanced degrees, including doctorates such as Ph.Ds, were acknowledged for their exceptional scholarly achievements, or were highly respected in their professional fields. Yet, all of them reported suffering from impostor feelings. (While Clance and Imes researched highly successful women, this phenomenon also affects men.) Impostor syndrome creates intense feelings of "the fear of being found out." It's a psychological pattern in which we don't believe that our skills, achievements, and successes are deserved. When we suffer from this syndrome, it can cause psychological distress, such as fear, anxiety, depression, shame, feelings of inadequacy, and self-doubt. Sometimes, we may feel like giving up because we hold irrational fears of the future. Despite evidence of our intelligence and competence, we think our success is due to luck and dismiss the opinions or admiration of others impressed with our intelligence, talents, and accomplishments. We distrust our capabilities and constantly compare ourselves to others. We may also dwell on the past and consistently engage in negative self-talk.

Impostor syndrome also controls how we react in certain situations and can limit our courage in pursuing our interests or new opportunities. For example, you might avoid applying for jobs if you don't meet every requirement, don't try out for sports, or decide not to join group activities at work, school, or in your community that you might otherwise enjoy.

When you feel undeserving or experience a sense of unworthiness about your accomplishments or current role, you tend to perceive yourself as an impostor and carry a profound fear of being unmasked as a fraud. This phenomenon isn't limited to introverts. Even those with extroverted, outgoing personalities who actively engage in their communities, workplaces, or social circles can grapple with it. They often rely on their charisma and unwavering dedication to shield their true selves from being exposed as impostors.

The article, "The Masks We Wear – Impostor Syndrome" published by *Illuminated Pathway,* captured this concept beautifully by stating, "It begins with knowing thyself. Most of us have forgotten who we are. Years of societal programming and wounding that begin early in childhood eventually cause us to lose touch with our true nature. We slowly accumulate layers of 'psychological armor' around our bodies that not only serve to shield us from the outer world, but keep us from accessing the inner world and the light that lives deep within our hearts and minds" (Schulz, n.d.).

In her book, *The Secret Thoughts of Successful Women*, Dr. Valerie Young (2011), a globally renowned authority on impostor syndrome and cofounder of the Impostor Syndrome Institute, delineated five well-defined "competence types" that encapsulate the effects and difficulties many of us experience with impostor syndrome.

- **"The Perfectionist":** This person believes they should consistently achieve flawless performance. When any aspect of their work isn't exemplary, falling short of 100 percent in quality and performance, it causes the Perfectionists to perceive themselves as failures, eliciting feelings of shame, according to Dr. Young's findings. Young says, "Some Perfectionists hold only themselves to these exacting standards, while others impose them on other people." When individuals fail to meet the high standards of a perfectionist, it often leads to frustration and disappointment. Dr. Young's research further explains that since perfectionists thrive on delivering stellar work and performance, anything less results in "harsh inner criticism" and "deep shame" at the potential of failure. This may result in avoidance of engaging in future or challenging projects because the risk of humiliation is too high. "Perfectionism is a hard habit to break because it's self-reinforcing. Because you do overprepare, you often turn out a stellar performance, which in turn reinforces your drive to maintain that perfect record. *But it's a huge setup.* Because when you expect yourself and your work to always be perfect, it's a matter not of *if* you will be disappointed but *when*," says Dr. Young.

- **"The Superhuman":** The Superhuman competence category can be mistaken for the Perfectionist. However, a significant distinction lies in the fact that the Superhuman excels at managing multiple roles masterfully. Both men and women in this category judge themselves harshly when they underperform, as noted by Dr. Young. She further explains that women often impose stricter expectations on themselves, evaluating their proficiency in handling multiple responsibilities both within and outside of work. The concept of "Superwoman" largely emerged as a cultural construct when the traditional role of a stay-at-home mother expanded to include the additional responsibility of being a full-time paid worker. Suddenly, the notion of "having it all" evolved into the expectation of "doing it all," according to Dr. Young's findings. She goes on to clarify that instead of attributing the pressure to balance their work and personal life solely to societal influences, individuals in this category convince themselves that true competence means being capable of proficiently managing every aspect of their lives.

- **"The Expert":** In contrast to The Perfectionist, who prioritizes the "quality" of work, Dr. Young refers to the Expert as "the knowledge version of the perfectionist." Experts place their emphasis on the "quantity" of knowledge or the level of skill they acquire, continuously seeking more knowledge, skills, and credentials without ever feeling satisfied. According to Dr. Young, the Expert believes that true competence and intelligence should enable them to retain knowledge or have the capacity to comprehend and recall everything they read. Dr. Young further explains that the Expert competence type tends to affect women more than men. Women often feel a compelling urge to continually accumulate additional education, credentials, and experience before considering themselves experts. "This relentless pursuit of more information, skills, and experience is what drives many people, especially women, to pursue additional and sometimes unnecessary training, degrees, or credentials," says Dr. Young. She continues to explain that this never-ending pursuit exacerbates impostor syndrome among women, leading them to believe they lack sufficient knowledge. This often results in delays in achieving their goals, sometimes spanning months or even years.

- **"The Soloist":** The Soloist often labors for years under the mistaken belief that genuine competence requires achieving success entirely independently, without any assistance, according to Dr. Young. She goes on to explain that this reluctance to seek assistance, advice, or coaching stems from the fear that it might be seen as a lack of expertise or knowledge, which in turn triggers feelings of shame. To some extent, the Soloist recognizes that the expectations placed upon them are frequently unattainable. However, they persistently push themselves to extremes, often at the expense of their health and personal life, in pursuit of what may seem like miraculous achievements. Dr. Young adds that throughout this journey, they persistently fear that, upon attaining success, others will view them as impostors barely hanging on and eventually realize that their abilities are not as extraordinary as they may have seemed.

- **"The Natural Genius":** This category of competence doesn't imply that the person is a genius. Instead, it highlights the belief that success depends solely on innate aptitude and intelligence. According to Dr. Young, individuals in this category believe that success should be effortless. "What a Natural Genius cares about the most is how and when accomplishments happen," she says. Her ongoing research reveals that individuals with a Natural Genius mindset tend to "set the internal bar impossibly high" by evaluating themselves based on ease and speed rather than flawlessness. They believe that success should come naturally. Furthermore, Dr. Young explains that Natural Geniuses expect to acquire knowledge without the need for formal instruction, to effortlessly attain excellence, and to achieve perfection from the outset. When faced with a situation that doesn't allow for quick or effortless achievement, their impostor syndrome is triggered, leading to a decrease in confidence. Dr. Young concludes that in such circumstances, Natural Geniuses take significant measures to avoid challenges due to the fear of failure, which generates feelings of shame if success is not achieved (Young 2011).

If you have any of these traits, they can severely limit you regardless of your level of success, as you continuously hold the belief that you may not possess the intelligence, creativity, or talent you project outwardly. This, in turn, reinforces the perception that you are undeserving of the hard-earned success you've worked so hard to attain.

In order to liberate yourself from the clutches of impostor syndrome, it's crucial to explore the root causes, which can encompass a range of factors, including childhood experiences, parental expectations, cultural or societal pressures, a competitive or demanding work environment, negative belief systems, or the belief that success or recognition is purely attributed to luck. Understanding these underlying causes can help you address and manage impostor syndrome.

Healing this syndrome often involves combining self-reflection, cognitive-behavioral therapy techniques, and building self-confidence to confront and transform your beliefs and thought patterns.

As you near the end of this chapter, you'll find Dr. Clance's Impostor Syndrome Scale[3], a tool crafted to help you assess whether you are experiencing the syndrome. Following that, a meditation will lead you in an exploration of the origins of your experience and the underlying beliefs that have triggered the syndrome. This process will empower you to discover a path to forgiveness for the individual or situation that may have been the source of the trauma. It's essential to bear in mind that the person responsible for the trauma may have been repeating behavior that was inflicted upon them.

---

[3] From *The Impostor Phenomenon: When Success Makes You Feel Like a Fake* (pp. 20-22), by P.R. Clance, 1985, Toronto: Bantam Books. Copyright 1985 by Pauline Rose Clance, Ph.D., ABPP. Reprinted by permission. Do not reproduce without permission from Pauline Rose Clance, drpaulinerose@comcast.net, www.paulineroseclance.com.

The last exercise will walk you through constructive healing steps to incorporate as you diligently work to release this syndrome and remember that you are worthy and deserving of everything you've accomplished. Alternatively, you might consider seeking the assistance of a trained therapist or coach who can offer guidance in breaking free from the overwhelming grip impostor syndrome may have on you. But for now, let's continue with Julie's story (introduced in Chapter 1).

Julie's Impostor Syndrome

Julie felt hopeless. She walked away from a successful, high-paying career with no specific plans. She was burned out and emotionally depleted after years of overextending herself, working long hours, and remaining in a job that provided a false sense of power but didn't feed her passion. Along the way, Julie had actually lost her passion and didn't know how to get it back. She reached a turning point in her life that forced her to look hard at herself and make radical changes.

The day she shared her story with me, I saw that the despair and exhaustion had taken over her mental, physical, and spiritual being. I didn't share my observations with her that day. It didn't feel like the right time because before receiving that feedback, she needed to heal and find the person she had lost.

One evening in late September, I sat at my desk, rubbing my eyes. It had been a long, stressful day. I thought about Julie and wondered how she was doing. Then, my thoughts were interrupted by a light knock on the door. I closed my eyes and prayed, "Dear God, please, no more issues today."

It was Julie. She looked radiant. It had been two years since she resigned.

"I know it's late. I hope you don't mind that I just dropped by. Are you up for dinner? My treat," she said.

"Absolutely. It's been one of those days. It'll be nice to have dinner with an old friend."

Julie and I sat in a back booth in a quiet restaurant. I started to speak when she put her hand up and said, "I want to thank you. The day I walked into your office, I was at the lowest point I'd ever been in my life. You were so kind to me, with no judgment. At the time, I didn't understand why you suggested journaling my feelings and finding forgiveness for people who have wronged me. I was so angry at everyone and everything. The last thing I wanted to do was relive the memories I was trying to forget."

"Did you journal your feelings?" I asked.

"Yes. I rented a small cottage on Martha's Vineyard and spent a lot of time sitting by the ocean. I did what you suggested and treated myself to a beautiful, leather-bound journal with an engraved dragonfly on the front. I remembered you telling me that dragonflies represent change. The words didn't come at first. I stared at the blank pages day after day. Finally, I was ready to give up, thinking journaling just wasn't for me. But then, I heard your voice, saying, 'Just start with one word that describes how you feel.' I wrote the word DESPAIR, and then I cried for two weeks. After that, the floodgates opened. I filled up three journals."

"What did you discover about yourself?"

"I always felt that I had to be the best at everything. I had to be perfect. I believed I needed to work harder than everyone else. I achieved my goals, but it was never enough. I would set higher, more challenging goals and achieve them. But I drove myself to exhaustion. The thought of failing made me feel anxious, humiliated, and ashamed."

"Julie, you've accomplished so much in your life. You should be proud of yourself."

"I know that now. I thought my parents would be proud of me. I never understood why they weren't. So, I worked harder. The more I achieved, the unhappier I became, and the guiltier I felt for having more than my family. They always compared my successes to the lack of success of my brothers and sisters. Remember when I called my parents to tell them I was engaged to Jonathan? Remember their reaction?"

I shook my head slowly, still in disbelief at how cruel her parents had treated her.

"I stopped sharing my successes with my family," Julie continued. "I got tired of feeling guilty, and the constant rejection was too much to handle. I haven't talked to them since the day I resigned. I remember that day so clearly. I felt like such an impostor. I believed if I didn't leave, I would be exposed."

I felt a nervous twinge in my stomach as I asked, "Exposed for what?"

"Exposed that I wasn't as intelligent and talented as everyone thought. That's why I walked away."

"Do you still feel that way?"

"Yes, a little bit. But I realized that my impostor syndrome stemmed from beliefs my parents conditioned me to believe about myself. I realized that I hid behind invisible masks my entire life. It's like changing your mask to fit the person or situation. It's no wonder I lost myself, lost my identity."

Julie sat back and took a long drink of her wine. I could see the little girl inside her. That look tugged on my heartstrings and brought me back to my own childhood memories.

"I received a call from an attorney two weeks ago," Julie continued. "My entire family was killed in a car accident. They were on their way to dinner when a tractor-trailer lost control. There were no survivors. That's why I'm in town."

I gasped. "Oh, my God, Julie. I'm so sorry!"

"There's more," Julie said matter-of-factly.

I poured more wine into each of our glasses. The waiter started to approach, but I smiled apologetically and put my hand up for him to wait. He nodded and turned back to the kitchen.

"Brenda, I found a key to a safety deposit box when I was going through my father's desk. I went to the bank and retrieved a large yellow envelope from the box."

"What did you find?"

She leaned forward with deep pain in her voice and whispered, "I don't think the people who raised me were my parents. I found an old skeleton key, a picture of a newborn baby, a birth certificate, and a letter from a woman I believe may be my biological mother."

"Is it a picture of you?"

"I don't know. I don't think so. I visited my grandmother and showed her what I found. But she refused to discuss it. Then, she slammed, locked the screen door, and walked back into the house. She left me standing on the porch."

"What are you going to do?" I asked.

"I'm going to find the truth. I need to know, Brenda. I need to know who I am. I've never felt like I belonged in my family. I always felt like an outcast, like I've been living someone else's life and afraid to show the world the true me. Do you understand what I mean?"

"Yes, I do. It feels like you're hiding behind invisible masks because you don't feel safe revealing your true authentic self. You feel pressured to conform to your family's or your company's values, beliefs, and behaviors even when it goes against your core. You continued until you lost sight of who you were because your fear of rejection was so intense that you hid behind the mask of inauthenticity. You subconsciously believed that you would face ridicule if you revealed your fears and weaknesses. I've seen these personality traits hundreds of times in my career and have experienced them myself."

"That's exactly it. You summarized what I have discovered about myself these past two years. I've wasted so many years believing I was an impostor, afraid of being discovered that I wasn't who I pretended to be so I'd fit in. Why did it take me so long?"

"I believe we're given our first mask as children. We wear them because we pine for our parents' love and attention. We become conditioned by our family, religion, cultural beliefs, and society, so we become proficient at conforming. We wear these masks to be what everyone expects us to be and forget they're just masks, not who we truly are. That's how we lose ourselves."

"That day I resigned, I woke up in the morning, stared at myself in the mirror, and didn't recognize the person staring back at me. Nothing mattered anymore—not my successful career, money, home, or relationships. Resigning was the best thing I ever did for myself. And I knew you understood. I could see it in your eyes."

"Julie, do you remember when we were kids that we couldn't wait to dress up for Halloween? How we picked our costumes? Do you know why we picked our favorite character? Because it was safe for us to hide behind a mask and become that character. We were able to forget about our self-limiting beliefs for one night. The costume made us feel happy, magical, beautiful, and, for some, unstoppable, like we possessed the powers of the character. This is why kids don't want to take their costumes off when they get home. They want to sleep in their costume to hold onto that feeling for as long as possible."

"I never thought about it that way. It makes sense."

"You mentioned earlier that you regret wasting so much time getting to where you are now. I want you to consider that you haven't wasted time. You're exactly where you need to be, and age doesn't matter. All your experiences brought you to the moment that helped you walk away and begin your healing journey. Unconsciously, you've carried around emotions that kept you imprisoned—sadness, grief, anger, insecurity, and resentment. It wasn't until you moved to Martha's Vineyard that you finally allowed yourself to feel. It takes great courage and self-love to heal and transition to higher consciousness. You should be proud of yourself. You're not the same person who walked into my office two years ago. I can see the change in you. Even in the face of this recent tragedy, you're doing remarkably well, and that is something to celebrate."

Julie's eyes glistened with tears as she raised her glass for a toast, "To me, then, and to you."

After we said our goodbyes, I walked back to my car, thinking about all the women who hid behind invisible masks, suffered from impostor syndrome, and feared revealing their true authentic selves. I know firsthand that removing our masks requires deep reflection.

We will discuss "Fear-less Authenticity" in Chapter 11, but for now, it's time to get out your journal and settle in for an exploratory exercise and healing meditation.

Dr. Clance's Impostor Syndrome Scale

CLANCE IP SCALE

For each question, please circle the number that best indicates how true the statement is of you. It is best to give the first response that enters your mind rather than dwelling on each statement and thinking about it over and over.

1. I have often succeeded on a test or task even though I was afraid that I would not do well before I undertook the task.

1	2	3	4	5
(not at all true)	(rarely)	(sometimes)	(often)	(very true)

2. I can give the impression that I'm more competent than I really am.

1	2	3	4	5
(not at all true)	(rarely)	(sometimes)	(often)	(very true)

3. I avoid evaluations if possible and have a dread of others evaluating me.

1	2	3	4	5
(not at all true)	(rarely)	(sometimes)	(often)	(very true)

Note. From The Impostor Phenomenon: When Success Makes You Feel Like A Fake (pp. 20-22), by P.R. Clance, 1985, Toronto: Bantam Books. Copyright 1985 by Pauline Rose Clance, Ph.D., ABPP. Reprinted by permission. Do not reproduce without permission from Pauline Rose Clance, drpaulinerose@comcast.net, www.paulineroseclance.com.

4. When people praise me for something I've accomplished, I'm afraid I won't be able to live up to their expectations of me in the future.

1	2	3	4	5
(not at all true)	(rarely)	(sometimes)	(often)	(very true)

5. I sometimes think I obtained my present position or gained my present success because I happened to be in the right place at the right time or knew the right people.

1	2	3	4	5
(not at all true)	(rarely)	(sometimes)	(often)	(very true)

6. I'm afraid people important to me may find out that I'm not as capable as they think I am.

1	2	3	4	5
(not at all true)	(rarely)	(sometimes)	(often)	(very true)

7. I tend to remember the incidents in which I have not done my best more than those times I have done my best.

1	2	3	4	5
(not at all true)	(rarely)	(sometimes)	(often)	(very true)

8. I rarely do a project or task as well as I'd like to do it.

1	2	3	4	5
(not at all true)	(rarely)	(sometimes)	(often)	(very true)

9. Sometimes I feel or believe that my success in my life or in my job has been the result of some kind of error.

1	2	3	4	5
(not at all true)	(rarely)	(sometimes)	(often)	(very true)

Note. From The Impostor Phenomenon: When Success Makes You Feel Like A Fake (pp. 20-22), by P.R. Clance, 1985, Toronto: Bantam Books. Copyright 1985 by Pauline Rose Clance, Ph.D., ABPP. Reprinted by permission. Do not reproduce without permission from Pauline Rose Clance, drpaulinerose@comcast.net, www.paulineroseclance.com.

10. It's hard for me to accept compliments or praise about my intelligence or accomplishments.

1	2	3	4	5
(not at all true)	(rarely)	(sometimes)	(often)	(very true)

11. At times, I feel my success has been due to some kind of luck.

1	2	3	4	5
(not at all true)	(rarely)	(sometimes)	(often)	(very true)

12. I'm disappointed at times in my present accomplishments and think I should have accomplished much more.

1	2	3	4	5
(not at all true)	(rarely)	(sometimes)	(often)	(very true)

13. Sometimes I'm afraid others will discover how much knowledge or ability I really lack.

1	2	3	4	5
(not at all true)	(rarely)	(sometimes)	(often)	(very true)

14. I'm often afraid that I may fail at a new assignment or undertaking even though I generally do well at what I attempt.

1	2	3	4	5
(not at all true)	(rarely)	(sometimes)	(often)	(very true)

15. When I've succeeded at something and received recognition for my accomplishments, I have doubts that I can keep repeating that success.

1	2	3	4	5
(not at all true)	(rarely)	(sometimes)	(often)	(very true)

Note. From The Impostor Phenomenon: When Success Makes You Feel Like A Fake (pp. 20-22), by P.R. Clance, 1985, Toronto: Bantam Books. Copyright 1985 by Pauline Rose Clance, Ph.D., ABPP. Reprinted by permission. Do not reproduce without permission from Pauline Rose Clance, drpaulinerose@comcast.net, www.paulineroseclance.com.

16. If I receive a great deal of praise and recognition for something I've accomplished, I tend to discount the importance of what I've done.

1	2	3	4	5
(not at all true)	(rarely)	(sometimes)	(often)	(very true)

17. I often compare my ability to those around me and think they may be more intelligent than I am.

1	2	3	4	5
(not at all true)	(rarely)	(sometimes)	(often)	(very true)

18. I often worry about not succeeding with a project or examination, even though others around me have considerable confidence that I will do well.

1	2	3	4	5
(not at all true)	(rarely)	(sometimes)	(often)	(very true)

19. If I'm going to receive a promotion or gain recognition of some kind, I hesitate to tell others until it is an accomplished fact.

1	2	3	4	5
(not at all true)	(rarely)	(sometimes)	(often)	(very true)

20. I feel bad and discouraged if I'm not "the best" or at least "very special" in situations that involve achievement.

1	2	3	4	5
(not at all true)	(rarely)	(sometimes)	(often)	(very true)

Note. From The Impostor Phenomenon: When Success Makes You Feel Like A Fake (pp. 20-22), by P.R. Clance, 1985, Toronto: Bantam Books. Copyright 1985 by Pauline Rose Clance, Ph.D., ABPP. Reprinted by permission. Do not reproduce without permission from Pauline Rose Clance, drpaulinerose@comcast.net, www.paulineroseclance.com.

Scoring the Impostor Test

The Impostor Test[4] was developed to help individuals determine whether or not they have IP characteristics and, if so, to what extent they are suffering.

After taking the Impostor Test, add together the numbers of the responses to each statement. If the total score is 40 or less, the respondent has few Impostor characteristics; if the score is between 41 and 60, the respondent has moderate IP experiences; a score between 61 and 80 means the respondent frequently has Impostor feelings; and a score higher than 80 means the respondent often has intense IP experiences. The higher the score, the more frequently and seriously the Impostor Phenomenon interferes in a person's life.

Exercise: Removing the Impostor Syndrome Mask Meditation

In the last two exercises, you've identified areas of your life you wish to change and the belief patterns that prevented you from moving forward. In this exercise, take some time to contemplate a situation or multiple instances in your life when your self-esteem or self-worth was significantly undermined. These experiences may have led you to question your capabilities, downplay your achievements, or nurture a lasting fear of being exposed as an impostor. In this meditation, you will meet your spirit guide, who will present you with a gift that brings you healing. You may want to record this meditation with some soft music.

Find a comfortable position where you won't be disturbed. Close your eyes, and center yourself by taking several deep, slow breaths.

---

[4] From <u>The Impostor Phenomenon: When Success Makes You Feel Like a Fake</u> (pp. 20-22), by P.R. Clance, 1985, Toronto: Bantam Books. Copyright 1985 by Pauline Rose Clance, Ph.D., ABPP. Reprinted by permission. Do not reproduce without permission from Pauline Rose Clance, drpaulinerose@comcast.net, www.paulineroseclance.com.

Imagine that you're walking on a cobblestone path. Beautiful trees and flowers surround you. The aroma of wild grapes and honeysuckle permeates the air, but as you look around, you don't see them. You stop to soak in the sun's warmth as you close your eyes and raise your head. A light breeze flows through your hair, and you feel safe. After a few moments, you hear a soft hint of chimes in the distance. Curious, you continue down the path until you approach an old rusty Winchester fence hidden by the brush. You're mesmerized by the beautiful details as you pull back the ivy and wonder what's on the other side.

You lift the latch, and to your surprise, the gate opens, and you walk through. Ahead, you see a path lined with old bricks. You walk under a wooden trellis covered with greenery. Honeysuckle and wild grapes drape over the top. You continue to walk through the manicured garden when you come to a stone bridge that crosses over a running creek. You step onto the bridge and notice someone sitting by a fire in the distance. As you get closer, you see a hue of colors surrounding him and realize he's your spirit guide. He stands and motions for you to join him. He tells you he's been anticipating your arrival.

You sit in front of the crackling fire, grateful for the warmth. He thanks you for coming, reaches into his robe, and hands you a small box. He nods for you to open it. You remove the lid, and within the box is a baby picture of you. Confused, you remove the photo and stare at it for a long moment before looking up at him. He tells you that your baby picture symbolizes that you were born in perfection, but you've lost sight of that because your heart is full of fear. You notice a larger box next to your chair. He nods for you to remove its lid. This box contains pictures of you throughout your years. As you thumb through the pictures, you ask why you wore different masks.

"Dear One," he explains, "The first picture of you wearing a mask was the day marked as the onset of your impostor syndrome. It was the day you made the choice to withdraw, becoming invisible, out of fear of being unmasked as an impostor. You concealed that aspect of yourself as a form of self-protection, driven by the belief that you were no longer genuinely competent, and by a deep-seated concern that others might discern your perceived imperfections."

You were afraid to show your true authentic self after that, so you hid behind masks. In your mind, that was the only way to survive. But the time has come for you to release these illusions and find forgiveness—forgiveness for yourself and forgiveness for the person who created this illusion. You can't hold yourself in darkness and expect others to see you in the light, Dear One."

A wave of emotions surfaces as you approach the fire. You hold the pictures in your hand, and as you begin to release each photo into the flames, you feel a deep sense of release as you watch each one disintegrate. You hold the last photo in your hand. It was the day you became invisible. You look up, and the person(s) who caused you the pain stands before you, asking for your forgiveness. You look at your spirit guide, and he communicates telepathically with you, saying, "Forgiveness will set you both free. They did to you what was done to them. It's time to heal and end this pattern so that it's never repeated again. Release this burden, Dear One, so you can return to wholeness."

You look into their eyes as you let the last photo fall from your hand into the fire. You feel the final release; with that, you forgive them and are ready to return to your authentic self.

Open your eyes and take a deep, cleansing breath.

What did you discover through this meditation? Can you identify the specific event or situation that led to the adoption of the impostor syndrome mindset? Which thoughts and emotions played a role in developing your impostor syndrome? Are you ready to let go of these misconceptions and work toward a sense of inner wholeness? Record these reflections in your journal.

Review the healing recommendations provided below. Following this exercise, rewrite your story to express your vision for the life you aspire to build and the specific actions you intend to undertake.

Exercise: Healing Impostor Syndrome

Healing impostor syndrome is a process that involves self-awareness, self-compassion, forgiveness, and adopting healthier beliefs, thought patterns, and behaviors. Here are some steps you can incorporate into your daily practice:

1. **Recognize and Acknowledge Signs of Your Impostor Syndrome:** The first step is to recognize and acknowledge that you are experiencing impostor syndrome. It's important to be honest about your feelings of self-doubt, inadequacy, and other impostor-related emotions such as anxiety, insecurity, and shame. Remember, this is not about judgment; it's about self-awareness and self-compassion. Impostor syndrome is a common phenomenon that plagues many people. When you experience these feelings, stop and recognize your inner dialogue with yourself. Determine which of the five competence types from Dr. Young's work best reflects your current thought pattern. Then, use this understanding to identify specific thought patterns and behaviors contributing to your impostor-related emotions. This awareness will serve as a foundation for challenging and changing these patterns, allowing for greater self-acceptance and confidence.

2. **Identify and Reframe Limiting Beliefs:** What negative beliefs immobilize you with fear and reinforce your impostor syndrome? What negative notions lead you to doubt your abilities? Do these thoughts have a factual basis, or are they distorted perceptions? Have you accepted someone else's viewpoint as an accurate portrayal of yourself? For each negative belief or thought you've identified, substitute it with a positive word or statement about yourself, such as

acknowledging that your accomplishments are valid and not merely the result of luck or chance.

3. **Prioritize Personal Validation Over External Validation:** It's essential to recognize that your worth isn't solely contingent upon external validation or the viewpoints of others. It starts with granting approval to yourself by valuing your own opinions and self-assessment. How frequently do you find yourself seeking external validation, approval, praise, or recognition from others to affirm your own abilities and achievements? When was the most recent occasion on which you acknowledged and validated your accomplishments independently, without relying on the opinions of others?

4. **Choose Self-Love Over Self-Judgment:** Treat yourself with the same kindness and understanding you would offer your best friend. Allow yourself the space to pursue wholeness and let go of self-limiting beliefs. Self-compassion means recognizing, embracing, and loving your imperfections. Choose empathy and care over harsh self-criticism. This practice is key to enhancing your mental and emotional well-being. Identify three self-compassion habits you can integrate into your daily routine. For instance, when you make a mistake, choose self-awareness and gratitude for the lesson learned instead of criticizing yourself. Respect your limitations—you don't need to master everything. Instead, focus on being resourceful and connecting with others who have the expertise you need. View each experience as an opportunity for growth.

5. **Embrace Your Limits: Set Realistic Expectations and Prioritize Self-Care:** Recognize that striving for perfection is an unattainable objective, and everyone is susceptible to errors. Set realistic expectations for yourself and embrace

the notion that it's perfectly acceptable to encounter setbacks or make mistakes. These experiences serve as opportunities for personal growth and expanding your knowledge. Review your "To-Do" list, and pinpoint areas where you're burdening yourself with excessive self-imposed pressure. What adjustments can you make to introduce more balance into your personal life? Not everything warrants top priority. Embrace your limits—understand that you don't need to manage every responsibility perfectly. Instead, delegate where possible, prioritize tasks that truly matter, and don't be afraid to say no when necessary. It's important to build in personal time for yourself. In the span of a year, there are 365 days, 8,760 hours, and 525,600 minutes. Make self-care a top priority and give yourself permission to dedicate time to your personal well-being.

6. **Genuinely Accept Compliments and Recognition:** When someone compliments you or recognizes your work, say, 'Thank you' instead of minimizing your achievements with self-deprecating remarks or apologizing to make someone else feel better, whether it's because you were in competition with them or because you want them to like you.

7. **Celebrate Your Achievements:** List ten of your achievements—no matter how minor and without passing judgment or engaging in negative self-talk—that you have never recognized or celebrated from your list. Afterward, determine how you will acknowledge these achievements and celebrate your efforts going forward, which will reinforce and nurture your self-confidence.

8. **Seek Support:** If you feel that accomplishing this on your own is too daunting, consider reaching out to a reliable therapist or counselor. They can provide guidance and

strategies to aid in your healing journey. Furthermore, support groups and mentorship connections can serve as valuable reservoirs of support and assistance.

Healing from impostor syndrome is an ongoing process that requires time to transform your mindset and nurture self-assurance. Remember that you are not alone in grappling with these emotions, and by developing self-awareness and seeking support, you can conquer impostor syndrome and flourish in both your personal and professional realms.

CHAPTER 5

STAYING ASLEEP: THE HIDDEN COST OF VICTIMHOOD

"My past does not define me; I am who I choose to be." ~ Unknown Author

Victim consciousness can be a sensitive topic to understand when you lack awareness of its emotional hold on your belief system and its impact on the quality of your life. It's a state of consciousness where you believe outside influences or people determine your destiny. It's a pattern that gives the illusion that you're powerless and that the path to freedom is to be saved or wait for others to change.

Victim consciousness often originates in childhood as a learned behavior from watching others or experiencing trauma. Children who are emotionally, sexually, and/or physically exposed to an abusive environment may develop self-defeating pathological behavior that correlates with the belief that they must suffer punishment in order to be loved.

They may also fear abandonment. When this happens, they lack coping skills and develop a negative victim mindset. Depending on the severity of emotional abuse, such as excessive parental criticism or neglect, overwhelming shame, or emotional deprivation, they might develop significant psychological issues. In some cases, this can contribute to the development of narcissistic personality traits in their later years.

When abused children become adults without awareness of their need to heal their deep-seated hurt and anger toward their parents or abuser, they can unconsciously remain in dysfunction because that's all they know.

This is not to say that everyone who experiences a tragic event develops a victim mentality. However, it's often a product of violence and a means to avoid criticism and responsibility by seeking attention and compassion for their situation in life. They do this because they're afraid to change, believing they will face more of the same, so they hold onto their story.

Others who don't experience abuse as a child can also slip into a victim mentality, feeling they have little control over their lives when they experience betrayal, continuous emotional pain, or other external situations. Since they believe they don't have the power to change their life, they take little or no action to improve their plight. If they embark on a healing journey, they must remove all excuses in order for the healing to occur and to evolve to higher consciousness. Otherwise, they will choose to remain asleep because it's easier and more familiar.

The Shadow

There is a shadow side to victim consciousness that is important to understand when embarking on a healing journey. The shadow has two sides: Dark and Light. The dark side is what we choose to keep hidden from the world, such as weaknesses, fears, emotional wounds, low self-worth, shame, or impulsive habits, which we try to ignore as long as we can.

When we choose not to face the dark shadow of victim consciousness, we often display several behaviors, such as manipulating others, ignoring unhealed emotions, or clinging to a sense of righteousness while continuing to feel persecuted by others or circumstances. Although our thinking and actions may be unconscious, it's easy to become a master manipulator as a form of survival.

This is tricky and difficult to heal without the awareness or guidance of a spiritual advisor or trained professional. This vicious cycle controls our need for attention, and because we haven't undergone proper healing, our ego maintains its grip on the belief that we need to continuously experience unjust and harmful events to get attention. When this happens, we create unhealthy scenarios (consciously or unconsciously) to garner ongoing sympathy, giving others the illusion that our life is a series of challenges beyond our control.

Our uncontrolled craving for pity and attention from others reinforces our ego-driven belief that we are victims. This victim identity provides a false sense of safety and comfort, allowing us to avoid feeling repressed emotions such as guilt, anger, shame, or other low-frequency, debilitating emotions. By doing so, we can continue evading responsibility for our lives and our impact on others.

As the dark shadow of victim consciousness intensifies, other detrimental personality traits can emerge. For example, a person might display passive-aggressive behavior, such as being critical, judgmental, or disparaging toward those close to them. When family members or friends stop tolerating this behavior, the individual's victim mentality can escalate. They may become more aggressive, combative, and defensive, refusing to listen or take accountability for their actions. To regain attention and sympathy, they might manipulate their loved ones by making them feel guilty or at fault, blaming them for various issues.

Since the victim must remain in control and is unwilling or incapable of apologizing, they manipulate situations and try to gain power over others, intending to tear down their loved ones by spewing accusatory and offensive remarks, hurtful insults, or unwarranted criticism.

In this way, they alternate between being the victim and the victimizer, deliberately hurting the people close to them or those trying to help. It's a vicious game that requires total control and manipulation of the situation on their part. Yet, they will cry out for help, often expecting their family members or friends to drop everything to come to their aid. They will exaggerate or dramatize an issue with the intent (consciously or unconsciously) to lash out at their helper. This behavior inflicts suffering and harm onto their friends or loved ones, as they secretly intend to convince their loved ones that their help only causes more damage and suffering.

When loved ones try to serve as rescuers or helpers, they may inadvertently enable the person to remain a victim, which then causes the rescuers to get sucked into the vortex of emotional abuse.

If you struggle with victim consciousness or have a loved one who does, it's essential to understand that you can choose to heal and transition to the light side of your shadow.

The light side of the shadow is when you're inspired to live a more authentic, fulfilling life and take full responsibility for your healing journey. This isn't an easy undertaking, and again, it often requires the help of a spiritual advisor or a trained professional who can gently guide you through the process of uncovering the experience that created the victim mentality. They can create a safe space for you to heal the old programming, reaching a new state of awareness. This is when a realignment occurs, and you begin to evolve from your lower ego mind to a state of neutrality, where your emotions shift from fear-based to the courage to embrace a new life.

As you integrate, you start to build a new, healthy life filled with happiness, freedom, peace, and loving relationships. The integration process begins with compassion, love, and forgiveness for yourself and others, and you realize your experience was part of your soul growth. This knowledge nourishes and empowers you to change your life while believing that you are worthy of living your destiny as you heal on a soul level.

I've coached both men and women with the victim mentality personality trait. People in relationships with them often feel like puppets on a string, wearing multiple masks and expected to change according to the victim's demands. Many stay in the relationship too long because they think they can change the victim. When that doesn't happen, they become "the abused" due to the victim's unresolved issues.

I lost a close friend named Autumn, who got involved with a man who hid behind many masks. We had been close friends for years, so there wasn't a day that we didn't talk or spend time together.

She was a strong-willed, opinionated, and independent woman. She also had a strong ego, so she rarely thought she was wrong. And when she knew she was wrong, her pride prevented her from apologizing.

When Autumn met Dean, she fell hard and fast in love with him. He made her the center of his life, showering her with expensive gifts, lavish getaway weekends, and the attention she never received from anyone else, especially her family. They dated for just six months before he asked her to marry him. Without hesitation, she said yes.

There was something about Dean that bothered me, however. The more time I spent with them, the more I realized he wasn't the person he portrayed himself to be. So I begged Autumn not to marry him so fast.

"I know everything I need to know about Dean," she countered. "We love each other. He's good to me. I want to have a life with him. I want to start a family."

"Autumn, you're only nineteen years old," I told her. "You've barely dated for six months. What's wrong with waiting a year so that you're sure you two are truly compatible?"

"Dean said you would try to stop our marriage. He said you were jealous. Why aren't you happy for me? I thought if anyone would be happy for me, it would be you."

"Jealous? Autumn, you know me better than that. I find that statement offensive, especially after all the years we've been friends. I'm happy for you. I just want to ensure you aren't rushing into anything you'll regret later."

"The only regret I have is not listening to Dean sooner about how you would try and tear us apart." Autumn slammed her coffee mug on the table and stormed out.

I knew there was no changing her mind. Her righteous attitude had always been her Achilles' heel.

Autumn and Dean married and honeymooned in Hawaii six months to the day after he proposed to her. She announced her pregnancy one month later. They both expressed excitement about becoming parents.

As weeks went on, I noticed changes in her demeanor. She rarely smiled, and her determination and drive were gone. She appeared nervous, unhappy, and timid. Her behavior mirrored how she was as a kid.

When I asked her what was wrong, she smiled weakly and blamed it on her pregnancy. I knew there was more to it, but I didn't dare press the issue. I was afraid she would pull away completely if I did.

As I feared, Autumn started to distance herself from me as the weeks passed. She waited several days to return my calls. When we spoke, it was brief. She always provided the same excuses for not calling sooner and needing to go—she was tired, busy, or Dean needed her.

A month before the baby was due, I saw Autumn in a grocery store. She looked exhausted. She had dark rings under her eyes, her swollen feet poured out of her shoes, and she looked like she had gained more than sixty pounds.

I walked up behind her. "Hey! How are you and Dean?" I said, smiling warmly.

"Oh, hi!" She said as she looked nervously down at her feet.

"I haven't heard from you for a while. I call, but you don't return my calls anymore.

"Yeah, I've been..."

"Busy. I know," I finished her sentence. "What happened to you, Autumn? I miss my friend."

"I'm sorry."

"I don't want you to be sorry. It doesn't matter. I'm just worried about you."

"Dean has been going through a rough time. He needs my attention," she said defensively.

"What about you? Isn't the baby due any day now?"

"Yeah. I'm fine, though. Listen, I need to get home. Dean is waiting for me to cook dinner. I forgot to pick up his beer yesterday. I'll give you a call soon!" she said as she rushed away.

I was disturbed and unsettled by Autumn's behavior. I stood there and watched her hurry through checkout and shuffle quickly to her car. We used to talk about everything, and now she was a complete stranger.

Six more months passed when I ran into Autumn's sister, Addison, at the Octoberfest in town.

"Addison, how are you? How's Autumn and Dean?"

"Brenda, it's good to see you. I'm doing well," Addison answered.

"I assume Autumn had her baby."

"Yes, a baby girl. She named her Sam."

"I always liked the name Samantha."

"No, her name is Sam because Dean was disappointed it wasn't a boy." Addison laughed as if to rationalize his disappointment.

I nodded and asked, "How are they doing?"

Addison shuffled her feet and smiled. I could see my questions made her uncomfortable, and I realized how similar her personality was to Autumn's.

"They're separated right now. Autumn and Sam are living with me."

I nodded again and kept eye contact with her. She looked around as if she was concerned Autumn would walk up any minute and discover what she had disclosed.

"I guess you'll find out eventually since it's all over town," she finally said. "Dean became emotionally abusive to Autumn shortly after returning home from their honeymoon. He showed sociopathic signs and was later diagnosed with Antisocial Personality Disorder and narcissism. Once Sam was born, he became even more aggressive."

"I'm so sorry to hear this, but thank you for telling me, Addison. Please let Autumn know my door is always open."

"I will, but you know how she is when someone thinks she's made a mistake."

I remembered that their father had been abusive—verbally at first, then physically. Autumn and Addison never learned how to love and respect themselves or set boundaries. They correlated love with abuse, which was a normal part of their lives. They learned to accept abusive treatment and believed their needs didn't matter, never learning self-love, self-respect, or self-worth. So, their beliefs of love and devotion aligned with the treatment they received. They simply didn't know any different.

Autumn internalized her rage and pain that she endured as a child, as well as the betrayal she felt from her mother who never stopped the abuse. This resulted in her life becoming self-destructive. Her passive-aggressive behavior toward others became more forceful. She became strong-willed, opinionated, and independent (a mask she wore well). When people disagreed with her or challenged her, she became argumentative, defensive, and verbally offensive to push them away so that they wouldn't see through her mask of self-judgment. It gave her a false sense of control by concealing her feelings of powerlessness.

When she met Dean, she didn't realize that she had attracted an abusive relationship similar to what she experienced while growing up. Her psychological profile contained deep-rooted, unresolved emotions of shame, self-blame, guilt, hopelessness, and despair. She attracted Dean into her life, fulfilling the need to remain the victim of abuse (conscious or unconscious). She was vulnerable to him because he created a façade that gave her false confidence, luring her into his narcissistic trap. Her desire for his unconditional love and attention stripped her mask away, revealing the personality traits she had kept hidden for years. This gave Dean an invitation to take total control over her.

Autumn's feelings of shame and unworthiness were amplified by the emotional abuse and conditioning she received from a man she loved and thought loved her. She stayed in the relationship, thinking she could change Dean and return him to the sweetness of their relationship when they dated. When Sam was born, Dean's condition worsened because all the attention went to Sam, not him. This stems from the fact that narcissists often lack empathy, engage in manipulative behavior, seek control, and seldom accept responsibility for their actions.

Autumn left Dean, thinking this threat would change him. Of course, he promised everything would be different if she returned with Sam, but that was just a ploy to get them back under his control. After they moved back home, his intense anger and aggression became volatile and physically abusive toward Autumn. He also alienated her from her family and friends. He made her feel invisible by shattering her self-esteem and self-worth.

I hoped Autumn would call me, but she didn't. She knew I would've helped her find a therapist to start her healing journey, but she chose to stay asleep, hide behind her dark shadow side, and cling to her victim ego. As an ego-driven victim, that mentality gave her a false sense of safety, comfort, and familiarity. It was easier to keep her repressed feelings hidden from others—her fears, secrets, shame, and feelings of unworthiness. Simply put, she wasn't ready to change.

Autumn knew I saw past the mask she was hiding behind. However, for her, the safer option was to end our long-standing friendship and sisterhood rather than confront her inner shadows and grant herself permission to heal, forgive, and transform her life. The path to healing and reconciling both the light and dark aspects of ourselves is essential for soul healing and returning to wholeness. Undertaking this journey demands great courage.

Sadly, Autumn endured the abuse for many years. On a particular Mother's Day, Dean returned home drunk. He started to beat Autumn when Sam jumped in to defend her mother. Dean turned on Sam, breaking her arm, punching her several times in the abdomen, and continuing to slam her head against the wall. Sam suffered from numerous contusions, a ruptured spleen, lacerations to her liver, and a subdural hematoma to the brain. The police arrested Dean, and both Autumn and Sam were taken to the hospital and treated. They released Autumn, but Sam remained in critical condition.

When I heard what happened, I wondered if almost losing her daughter at the hands of the man she thought she loved would finally prompt Autumn to awaken. I visited Sam at the hospital, hoping to see my friend. When I walked into Sam's room, Autumn was sitting beside the bed, holding her daughter's hand and crying softly. I wasn't sure what reception I would receive, but I needed to try one more time.

"How is she?" I asked quietly.

Startled, Autumn looked up. I stood close to the door waiting for her to speak.

"What are you doing here?" Autumn asked.

"I heard about Sam and thought . . . well, I thought you might need a friend."

Autumn stood slowly, carefully releasing Sam's hand. Her daughter lay unconscious with a swollen face, bruises, and white gauze covering her head.

When Autumn walked toward me, I noticed her face was swollen, too, with black and blue bruises covering most of it. A deep cut with several stitches sat above her right eye. Her upper lip was split open, and her left cheek bled through a large Band-Aid. I felt enraged seeing her so vulnerable, scared, and broken. I kept my facial expressions neutral and my body relaxed, but inside, my heart pounded. I could feel my blood pressure rise. I wanted to inflict the same pain on Dean that he had inflicted on these two beautiful souls.

Autumn stood in front of me now. I didn't know what to expect. She looked so fragile as if a strong wind could blow her away. "Do you need a friend?" I asked softly.

She slowly placed her arms around my waist and rested her head on my shoulder as she sobbed uncontrollably. I held her and let her cry.

"It's going to be okay. I'll help you through this if you want." I whispered.

She continued to cry as I held her. I didn't move, allowing her tears to saturate my shirt.

"I can't believe you came, especially after how I've treated you. I'm so sorry."

"That's in the past. Let's focus on now. What do you say?"

She nodded and released her grip.

I stayed at the hospital for several hours. I asked if she wanted to move in with me until she figured things out, but she declined. She was happy at her sister's.

Sam remained in the hospital for four months until they transferred her to a rehabilitation center. The court sentenced Dean to ten years in prison. He had a lengthy criminal record for similar charges from his previous marriages. Autumn didn't even know he'd been married five times before. When the Sergeant revealed this information, I saw something change in her eyes. "I hope this information is finally enough for her to take back her life," I thought.

Autumn finally went through years of therapy, exploring her belief systems, finding forgiveness, and learning to love herself unconditionally. She and Sam are now actively involved in not-for-profit organizations that help battered women. They volunteer their time at women's shelters and programs to help women start new lives, and they serve as role models and mentors to women, teens, and children. Through their darkness, they found light and purpose.

Victim Mentality Assessment

Victim mentality is an acquired personality trait that often originates from childhood conditioning. This may result from sustaining some form of abuse during childhood—whether physical, sexual, emotional, or psychological. Even if you weren't a victim of abuse, you might have lived with or had a codependent relationship with someone who exhibited a victim mentality. This awareness is not about placing blame but shedding light on the roots of these patterns so you can begin a transformative journey toward healing and empowerment.

To further your journey of self-discovery, consider taking the Victim Mentality Assessment, which you'll find the link below. This assessment will provide valuable insights into your tendencies and reveal their impact on your emotional health and relationships.

When I engage in self-discovery exercises, I like to begin with a prayer to approach the process with ease, grace, and healing: *I invoke the beautiful divine light to shine within me and reveal the areas of darkness that keep me functioning as a victim. May I recognize these truths with compassion, have the courage to take accountability for change, and have the perseverance to return to wholeness. And so it is.*

To explore whether you are operating from a victim mentality, take the free Victim Mentality Assessment available at https://brendahukel.com/assessment.

Breaking Free from Victim Mentality

1. **Acceptance and Acknowledgment:** Reviewing your assessment results and recognizing your tendency toward a victim mentality can be challenging. However, this awareness and acknowledgment are crucial first steps toward transforming the thoughts and behaviors that keep you feeling powerless or cause you to blame others. It allows you to identify the fear-based behaviors that keep you trapped in a victim mindset or tied to past trauma, experiences, or stories.

2. **Roots of Victim Mentality:** In Chapter 3, we explored belief systems and conditioning, providing insight into the wounds that keep us as unconscious victims. As you work through

these emotions, remember that to change and break free from these debilitating patterns, you must let go of blame, judgment, and other toxic emotions that keep you in a victim mentality. This requires compassion and forgiveness for both yourself and others. Holding on to anger, resentment, revenge, or hate is like drinking poison and expecting your enemy to die. I will cover forgiveness in Chapter 8.

3. **Positive Reinforcement:** Be mindful of the negative words, beliefs, and deliberate actions you engage in daily. If this is difficult for you, review your past journals. What words did you use? How often did you judge yourself or someone else? What themes are most prevalent? Did you express gratitude for your blessings, or are your entries filled with toxic emotions? Each time you say something negative, find judgment, feel sorry for yourself, or want to tell your story, stop, take a deep breath, and replace it with a positive affirmation. Make a list of ten to fifteen things you're grateful for, and sincerely feel the gratitude either before bed or when you wake up in the morning. This practice will help you recognize and appreciate the many positive aspects of your life, reinforcing a more uplifting perspective.

4. **Stay Present:** A victim often lives in the past and future, dwelling on past grievances and fearing future injustices. Stay present and envision yourself achieving your goals. Visualize the person you want to become, and keep that image in your heart and mind. Find a picture representing your ideal self and place it somewhere you'll see it often.

5. **Respect and Kindness:** When you're stuck in a victim mentality, you focus on yourself with little regard for the negative impact you may have on others and often expect something in return. Practice respect and kindness. Do something

special for your loved ones, be mindful of their needs, and refrain from manipulating them for personal gain. These acts of kindness will help you shift away from self-centeredness and build healthier, more loving relationships.

6. **Accountability:** Taking responsibility for your healing allows you to make different choices and empowers you to transform your life and realign with your true self. This requires us to stop telling our story in search of sympathy from others. We must refrain from judgment, criticism, and self-pity. Instead, focus on the courage you have to change your life. Use affirmations or "I AM" statements, such as: "I lovingly forgive and release my past" or "I AM empowered to create a life that brings me peace, joy, and happiness." By reciting affirmations or "I AM" statements, you will begin to reprogram your subconscious mind, reminding yourself that you're a warrior, not a victim.

7. **Consistency:** Healing a victim mindset is a continuous process. Stay committed to your growth by consistently applying the insights and practices you've learned.

CHAPTER 6

THE VIBRATIONAL DANCE OF LIGHT AND DARK FREQUENCIES

"Our vibrational frequency is the language through which we communicate with the universe." ~ Brenda Hukel

According to quantum physics, everything is energy. Your thoughts, feelings, and words hold a vibrational frequency that is either positive or negative. The universe doesn't distinguish between the two. Its job is to deliver experiences based on your belief system, which determines your frequency level.

The Law of Attraction maintains a nuanced perspective that delves into how the magnetic force of your thoughts exerts a profound influence, shaping the very trajectory of your life. Your thoughts, in essence, serve as the master sculptors of your reality. This profound concept traces its roots back to the 19th century and has transcended time as a focal point of reflection across a wide range of cultures revered by philosophers and imbued within the teachings of spiritual masters.

When you have feelings of happiness, gratitude, and love within you, they act as beacons, attracting matching energies into your life. The opposite is also true. If you emit frequencies of anger, fear, hate, shame, anxiety, or rage, the universe responds in kind, orchestrating experiences that perpetuate that same vibrational realm. The universe remains attuned to the energetic choices that keep you locked in that vibrational vortex, whether positive or negative. You decide.

This is a difficult concept to understand when your life is in shambles. The question goes back to your beliefs: What are you thinking, feeling, or verbalizing? What invisible masks are you hiding behind to mask your emotions?

As mentioned in Chapter 5, you have both dark and light shadows. You can't experience one without the other. For example, your ego plays a tape in your mind that you are a victim of circumstances, representing your dark shadow. Your light shadow plays a different tape that you survived the trauma and are now creating a new life of happiness, health, and wholeness.

Your dark shadow controls the side of you that you don't want others to see. You may bury your experiences, traumas, or emotions so deeply that it's hidden from your conscious mind until you experience an emotional trigger. When you're triggered, your subconscious mind takes over, your ego engages, and you react to situations that threaten to reveal the secrets and fears you fight to keep buried deep within your psyche. Depending on who you're with or the situation that unfolds, you decide which to engage in—light or dark. It's a delicate dance.

By avoiding your shadow, you will continue to attract people and situations into your life that reflect your inner world. Healing your shadow side isn't something that should be taken lightly, however. It requires brutal honesty, awareness, and the courage to slowly peel away each layer so that you can heal, become the person you long to be, and live the life you desire.

As you work to integrate your shadows, the new energy will cause disruptions to help you release the old programs and become the "observer" of your life. This awareness undergoes deep healing by coming out of the darkness into the light. The observer understands the importance of stepping out of a situation that triggers you, recognizing the value of the lesson rather than reacting defensively and allowing the negative emotions to consume you.

When someone triggers you, it isn't about them. They're simply serving as a teacher to reveal an aspect of your consciousness that needs healing. Let's say you experience constant disappointment from people in your life. The disappointment is an emotional trigger alerting you that this belief needs to be released and healed. When this happens, ask yourself, "What would I need to believe about myself to keep experiencing disappointment and heartbreak? How am I creating (consciously or unconsciously) this repeated pattern? Am I holding a belief that I'm unworthy or undeserving of a healthy, loving relationship?"

This reality teaches you awareness and raises your consciousness. You learn to breathe into your higher consciousness and make a decision to choose differently. Breathing through it allows alignment to take place. You do this by returning to a state of neutrality and becoming the observer of your life vs. choosing to remain the victim and creating more negative experiences. Staying in the neutral zone allows your mind, body, and behavior to align and operate as one.

When you become a skilled observer, you'll recognize that the person who triggered you mirrors something that requires healing within you. In that way, they provide you with a gift. This can't happen when your ego is engaged because your defenses are up, and you're afraid to surrender to your healing. When the memory, person, experience, or trauma no longer triggers you, you've reached a level of awareness and healing that opens the door for you to embark on your spiritual awakening and ascend to higher consciousness.

Your higher self will continue to bring experiences into your life, revealing parts of your belief system that need to be transformed and evolved to a higher frequency—a higher consciousness. If you ignore these healing opportunities, the energy can manifest through dysfunctional relationships, addictions, mental illness, or chronic health issues.

Your body is a perfect barometer for alerting you when you're out of balance or harboring deep-seated emotions. When this happens, you'll manifest physical symptoms. Louise Hay (1984), *New York Times* bestselling author and founder of Hay House, wrote in her book, *You Can Heal Your Life*, that there is a direct correlation between dis-ease and emotions.

Healing your dark shadow is crucial to transitioning to a higher consciousness so that you can experience love and acceptance toward yourself and others. To embark on this courageous journey, you must explore the trauma or event that keeps you functioning at the lowest level of consciousness—fear, shame, guilt, hate, sadness, anger, jealousy, and grief. By healing the trauma, you'll experience freedom and alignment with your higher consciousness, release your dark shadow, and transition back into your authentic self.

When you integrate your shadows, you're transitioning from a third to fourth-dimensional reality because you're evolving from your lower ego mind to your heart mind. This state of neutrality moves you from fear-based frequency to a state of awareness of knowing vs. being. In this state, you learn to start trusting in divine timing and understand the power of surrender. You become the observer of your life.

Before achieving this level, you need to be comfortable with being uncomfortable because the integration process will cause disruption. This disruption is necessary for a new, high-vibrational frequency to emerge from the dark shadow, allowing old programming to reach a new state of awareness for healing.

As you clear the darkness, be prepared for people to be removed from your life because as you increase your frequency, they won't be able to tolerate the vibrational frequency from which you're operating. Situations will also intensify so that you can clear the old energy. It's important to remember that this transformation is not happening *to* you but *through* you. Refrain from judgment, and allow everything to unfold naturally. Remember to practice deep breathing during this transition. Again, breathing allows alignment to take place. It's about efficiency, not speed. Your belief system will be challenged, and everything will shift as you transition out of the dark and into the light shadow. The transition must be done with ease and grace so that your body can adjust to the new energy. To operate in higher consciousness, you'll need to have unwavering trust and the ability to surrender the outcome. This is when you'll experience miracles and the power of synchronicity.

Let's look at Olivia's situation. For years, she carried deep-seated anger toward her husband and believed he betrayed her when he filed for divorce. It wasn't until she worked with a holistic therapist that she realized she blamed her husband for her unhappiness. She chose to wear the wounded mask, and she wasn't able to distinguish between her beliefs and reality. Her lack of discernment kept her in the low vibrational energy of judgment.

Her husband served as a mirror to her because he ended the marriage to find happiness. When she worked with her therapist to explore her shadows, she realized her anger wasn't really at her husband but at herself because she was jealous—he changed his life and found happiness. She didn't. She also discovered that the second mirror was her betrayal of herself by remaining a wounded victim.

As you'll recall, in Chapter 3, Olivia insisted on filing a retaliation complaint against her boss, Royce, for assigning her one of the company's largest accounts. The emotional trigger she experienced stemmed from her belief that she was a victim of circumstances (the victim mask). During her therapy sessions, she realized that the emotional trigger and overreaction came from a deep-rooted childhood experience that she was expected to carry someone else's responsibility yet again. This shadow created a deep wound repeating the same patterns because of the low vibrational energy she kept putting out into the universe. Remember that the universe doesn't distinguish between positive and negative. It simply reacts to the strength of our vibrational frequency.

Olivia further uncovered feelings of immense guilt and shame that originated the day her mother died. After two years in therapy and integrating her shadows, she experienced a radical reawakening. She found her voice, took her power back, and changed her life to be what she secretly desired—freedom, empowerment, self-worth, happiness, and living her true purpose.

She went back to college to become a certified holistic therapist. She realized all the people in her life played critical roles that made her the woman she is today—a successful, well-respected therapist in her community. Without experiencing the darkness, she couldn't have experienced the light. She removed the victim mask and took responsibility to change and heal her life. She also reached a point in her therapy in which she forgave all the people in her life who played a critical role in fulfilling their soul agreements with her.

Exercise: Emotional Remapping

In previous exercises, you reviewed your belief systems and identified when you were operating as a victim. You'll use this information to explore your dark shadow, remove old programs, and increase your vibrational frequency. Let's begin with a prayer.

Prayer: *I invoke the divine spirit to submerge my shadow side with healing light. Guide me through this integration process with grace and ease as I heal and release old programming, perceptions, and judgments that prevent me from living authentically. Amen.*

1. In reviewing your responses to previous exercises, what are the top three emotions that keep you operating in a low vibrational frequency? For example, are they fear, mistrust, victimization, anger, blame, hate, disappointment, shame, etc.?

2. Where did each of these emotions originate? Are they generational? Did they originate from your mother or father or their parents? Were they from a trauma, death, etc.?

3. What program is running in the background that keeps you in a low vibrational frequency? For example, you might be running one of these programs in your mind: "No one cares about me. They only care about what I can do for them. I have to work so hard at everything that I don't have time to enjoy my life. I need complete control to prevent others from seeing through my façade. I can't express how I truly feel. I have to be perfect, so no one sees my flaws."

4. Based on these beliefs, what are your emotional triggers? How do people trigger you? How do you react when triggered? Go deep until you get to the root of the belief that causes the trigger.

Change can only come from within you. The first step is awareness of how you have betrayed yourself with your beliefs, emotions, and behaviors. It's difficult, if not impossible, to heal when you're in survival mode. To transition from low-level consciousness, you must remove the old programs that are running your life. To do this, here are four essential steps:

1. **Acceptance:** When you accept your current state with love, you can release the version of yourself you created to survive.

2. **Compassion:** When you hold yourself and others in compassion, your belief system shifts, and the negative dialogue/programs you're running in your mind will start to disintegrate.

3. **Allowance:** When you allow your authentic power to come through, you can operate from a higher vibration, which is your original state or simply, love. Then, you will switch from being the victim to being the observer of your life.

4. **Gratitude:** Understanding and expressing gratitude for the people who played a role in your life is essential for your healing. They fulfilled their agreement with you, so you can now

release them with grace and ease. If you release them with the same negative emotions you have felt in the past, the energy you have attached to them will return to you. (We will discuss "The Sacred Bonds of Soul Contracts" in Chapter 7.)

As you work through this process, the universe will surface old, outdated programs until you heal and release them. Some of the programs may be intense. It just means they are ready to be transformed. Breathe through the intensity and say, "Thank you for bringing this into my awareness for clearing. I invoke my higher self to clear this debris out of my consciousness with ease and grace. Thank you. Thank you. Thank you."

Each time you ask your guides to clear the debris from your unconscious programming, you move into a state of neutrality and become the observer. A realignment takes place and puts your ego on notice that you're in charge now and are healing all that blocks your integration.

When you're at the end of an old program, your ego will try to pull you back because it doesn't want you to grow. It wants you to keep searching so that you stay in linear, fear-based thinking, feeling there's no way out. Fear-based thinking keeps you fixated on the past and fearful of the future.

During this phase, stay mindful of your mental and verbal vocabulary. For example, saying, "I'm stuck, I'm done, I've had enough, or I don't know what to do anymore" will keep you in the old program of self-judgment, frustration, and despair. This is a third-dimensional reality ruled by fear. You can't elevate to higher consciousness while staying in the third dimension. Remember that words carry vibrations. What you put out is what you'll get back.

Replace your verbiage with high-frequency statements such as, "I am strong, resilient, and successful in everything I do. I am open to receiving all that I need to heal. I am a powerful being. I am open to receiving unconditional love for myself. I lovingly release people who no longer align with my vibrational frequency."

Declarations such as these automatically notify the universe that you're creating a new paradigm. You're no longer agreeing to remain unconscious; you're choosing self-mastery, empowerment, and alignment with your higher self.

Congratulations on reaching this point in the book. You're doing great! Take your time with this exercise. Follow the four practices above and remember to breathe through the underlying emotions and beliefs. Breathing helps move the energy through you.

CHAPTER 7

THE SACRED BONDS OF SOUL CONTRACTS

"Soul contracts are the lessons hidden within life's moments, as wisdom unfolds." ~ Brenda Hukel

There are many beliefs about our journey to earth and what happens to our souls after we die. Raised Catholic, I was taught we only live one life and that there is no such thing as reincarnation. I was also taught that if we break a commandment, we face damnation unless we confess our sins to a priest. I never understood why we needed to confess to a priest when we could pray directly to God.

My religious training also taught me that we face judgment day when we die to determine if we're righteous enough to be allowed into heaven. But most of us go to purgatory, a place of suffering inhabited by sinners who must expiate their sins first. I was taught that we spend eternity in hell if our souls don't enter purgatory to be cleansed of our sins and achieve holiness to enter the gates of heaven. The religion drilled into me was fear-based and controlling.

We live in an imperfect world, yet we're expected to be perfect or spend the rest of our lives fearing that hell awaits us on judgment day. Our God is supposedly all-forgiving and all-loving, so to believe that we'd spend eternity in hell because we died before repenting of our sins is absurd. What happened to all the poor souls who lost their lives during COVID-19 in 2021 while the churches were closed? Were they automatically condemned to hell because they couldn't confess their sins to a priest before they crossed over?

I believe in God and the angelic realm. However, I don't feel religion should be fear-based, nor should we be taught that we're unworthy and will face damnation if we don't adopt religious belief systems that are designed to control us and keep us in fear.

Many religions don't believe in reincarnation, yet thousands of past life regression cases have shown that people under hypnosis can travel back to different lifetimes. These regressions have revealed the origins of their phobias, illnesses, fears, and anxieties and have helped them experience profound healing in their current lives.

One of the most renowned pioneers in history, Brian L. Weiss, M.D., a prominent American psychiatrist and a distinguished figure in history, substantiated the importance of reincarnation through his extensive research focused on past life regression, reincarnation, and future life progression.

Another well-researched theory is that when we reincarnate, we choose the people and experiences we need for our soul growth. The first time I came across this concept, I was resistant to it. I wondered why on earth I would choose the life I chose. It wasn't until I realized that my fear and religious training kept my mind closed to the possibility that this could be true.

Our fear causes us to close our minds to possibilities outside of our generational belief systems. The vulnerability of exploring new concepts and opinions would risk ridicule and rejection from our inner circle. As you will learn in Chapter 12, part of the awakening process is to break out of our third-dimensional, fear-driven consciousness to align with

Christ Consciousness, which is pure love. We can't awaken if we remain in fear and ego-based consciousness.

This understanding permitted me to explore the unfamiliar. If it felt right in my heart, not my head, I remained open as I pieced together these new concepts, theories, and studies on my quest to awaken and align with Christ.

Exploring the possibility that we've lived multiple lifetimes may take some time, but have you ever met someone and felt like you knew them before or visited a place that felt familiar even though you'd never been there? How do you explain a child, who sits at a piano and plays Mozart perfectly without ever having a lesson? The child may have been a pianist in a previous lifetime. How do you explain your deep phobias without experiencing the trauma that caused the phobia in this lifetime?

I have now come to believe that everyone who touches our lives agrees to play a role in our soul development. A homeless man teaches gratitude, an alcoholic may teach the value of life, an abuser teaches forgiveness, and someone who betrays us teaches us self-worth and strength. Abandonment teaches us to survive on our own. There are numerous reasons and lessons, all of which are part of our soul contract.

I have conducted extensive research on reincarnation and how we choose our soul groups. I found that we carefully select our experiences, surroundings, and relationships on a soul level to help awaken and ascend to higher consciousness—a state of being of pure love and enlightenment. I had many questions about this concept, such as how life's trauma brings us to a state of love and why we would choose a life filled with pain and hardship. The answers were consistent: we determine what our soul needs to evolve. Some people in our lives will be there for a short time, others for an extended period, and some for multiple lifetimes. However, we have free will and can choose whether to accept life's lessons and continue growing or remain stagnant as we succumb to our circumstances.

Our soul agreements and the people who agree to contribute to our primal wounds are critical in helping us discover who we're destined to become in our current life. When we complete each phase of our journey, we evolve to the next level, releasing the patterns that brought us to this point in our healing. Once we fully ascend, we'll never return to the person we were before that experience.

Imagine sitting in the audience with everyone you agreed to incarnate with, watching the premiere of your soul movie. Like the Disney movie *Soul*⁵, the actors in your soul movie act out scenes for you to discover your true path as you walk through the darkness and the light of each experience. Each of these experiences is part of your divine plan. They show you what needs healing to evolve to higher consciousness, removing the invisible masks that no longer serve you. As the film ends and the curtains close, you realize you're no longer the character you played at the beginning of your movie because you've transformed. You've awakened and are ready to transition to the next phase of your journey.

As you'll discover in Chapter 11, part of the awakening process is to come to a place of pure love by embracing your true self and experiencing fearless authenticity. This is the purpose of a soul contract, even though some soul contracts create painful traumas and hardships. These traumas and hardships are experiences that force us to recognize the deep-seated wounds we must heal on a soul level in order to transform and expand our consciousness. When we do, we transition from the third-dimensional consciousness into the fourth dimension until we've reached self-mastery—the fifth dimension.

To initiate the awakening process, we form multiple soul agreements to experience the light and dark. We can't have one without the other; this is called duality. We will continue encountering hardships and challenges until we've reached our inner light and choose to embrace the lessons of our soul contract with gratitude and deep understanding that those lessons were vital for our ascension. When

---

[5] *Soul*, directed by Pete Docter (2020; USA: Disney+, Walt Disney Studios Motion Pictures), Theatrical.

we're in the fourth-dimensional reality, we're still operating in duality. Our consciousness starts to awaken, and our desire to conform to fit in dissipates because the need for authenticity is more important. It's during this process that we begin to see the world through the eyes of gratitude, love, and trust.

Nevertheless, the fourth-dimensional process is challenging and can create pain, suffering, and chaos. This is unavoidable because we've embarked on a healing journey. We must confront our inner demons and heal from the inside out. The more authentic we become, the more vocal we'll be because we need to connect to something bigger than our linear thinking. To reach this state of self-awareness and view the world with love, joy, and compassion vs. lack, separation, and judgment, we must recognize that the reward will outweigh the pain of the transition. This process, of course, takes great courage and perseverance.

Our soul agreements can take on many forms for us to embrace the lessons we need to learn. If one of our soul agreements is to learn forgiveness, how can we understand the value of it without being deeply hurt? When we experience the reason to forgive, we can choose to remain the victim of circumstances, allowing our heart to cling to the anger, resentment, and revenge, or we can choose to forgive. When we do, we don't pretend that the abuser's actions were okay, nor do we have to stay in the relationship or situation, opening ourselves up to more pain. We forgive the abuser, with whom we signed a soul contract, so that we can set ourselves free and complete the agreement we made with them. (Refer to Chapter 8 for more on forgiveness.)

If, for example, our soul agreement is to learn how to become a strong, independent woman, we might agree to be betrayed, abandoned, or abused in our life until we master the lessons to transform. With these experiences, we always have two choices: remain the wounded victim or integrate our shadows. Integration of our dark and light shadows allows us to regain our power and experience freedom because we understand the value of the lessons we endured.

As mentioned earlier, I experienced a life filled with abusers. I gave my love and loyalty to people and continuously faced betrayal, judgment, and pain. It took me more than fifty years to understand what I'm sharing with you today. I felt I had wasted many years of my life. I always stood alone in the world, weathering the storms by myself. Through their treatment, the people in my soul group taught me to stand in my integrity regardless of the challenges and heart-wrenching experiences I suffered. Without those experiences, I wouldn't be the strong, independent woman who survived the harshest of conditions. For me to ascend to higher consciousness in this lifetime, my lessons have been forgiveness, self-love, and self-worth. This isn't an easy contract by any means, but an important one for me to embrace the lessons for my spiritual and soul growth.

Soul agreements help us heal as we live through the Dark Night of the Soul. Our experiences and the careful crafting of our soul contracts and relationships guide us on a journey to awaken our capacity for unconditional love for ourselves and others. Each path is different and determines what soul lessons most benefit our growth. Ultimately, however, it's all about evolving to Christ Consciousness, which, again, is pure, unconditional love—the fifth-dimensional reality we'll discuss in Chapter 12.

Of course, we may also have souls in our life who show us love, kindness, and self-acceptance. They may serve as earth angels to guide us on our journey to self-discovery and self-love. Either way, everyone in our life serves an important role. It's what we decide to do with the lessons that matters most. We can own them and evolve to attract more love or remain wounded and attract more of the same experiences. We have the free will to choose. If we avoid the lessons in our current lifetime, we may return to learn the same lessons in another lifetime. This is a universal law.

Our experiences can also put us on a path that leads us to a higher purpose, which impacts others' lives. Look at all the organizations originating from someone who had a traumatic life experience and channeled their energy to helping others vs. staying the wounded victim. On a soul level, they agreed to a horrific experience in order to help others heal and regain their life. As a result, they touch the lives of hundreds or thousands.

I've watched people hide behind their trauma or hardships because of shame, anger, jealousy, righteousness, or other debilitating emotions without understanding the concept or value of soul agreements. Without the proper guidance, their true selves remain hidden behind their invisible masks, and they fail to channel their experiences or have the courage to see, embrace, and learn to love their authenticity. It's common for people to stay in a state of righteousness and not forgive because of their trauma. However, studies of past life regression indicate that the lessons we choose to learn in our present lives may be the same offenses we committed in another lifetime.

Once we've completed the phases of our integration process, the universe will test us by delivering more intense lessons through different scenarios. If there's no emotional trigger, that lesson is healed and no longer has power over us. We then feel the shift within us. If we don't feel the shift (a sense of freedom, peace, forgiveness, or release), more work is required, and that's okay. The soul contracts don't end until we've learned the lessons we've agreed to learn. Once we do learn the lessons, the universe removes the people from our lives because they've fulfilled their contractual promises to us. This cycle continues, and new people appear as we advance on our spiritual journey to higher consciousness.

Since everyone has free will, however, not everyone will embark on a spiritual awakening. I have witnessed many cases of people who exercised their free will to resort back to their old ways because, as dysfunctional and unhealthy as their life was for them, it was familiar. They decided not to awaken, heal, or ascend. They chose to remain asleep.

Autumn exercised her free will after she was submerged in the absolute throes of darkness. It wasn't until her husband severely beat Sam that she finally chose to change her life and begin her healing journey/awakening. Dean agreed to serve as an abusive narcissist who was vindictive and abusive emotionally and physically, showing no empathy or remorse for his treatment toward her or Sam. Instead, he was critical and accusatory, taking no accountability for his actions. This soul agreement forced Autumn to determine what she needed to heal. For many years, she chose not to transform her belief system. Instead, she repeatedly returned to her old life because it was familiar and comfortable, even though Dean was dangerous. As dysfunctional and unhealthy as it may sound, she knew what to expect and believed she didn't deserve a better life. She also had contracts with her parents, as her father abused her, and her mother felt incapable of protecting her.

Based on the soul agreement, Sam gave Autumn unconditional love and needed her mother to protect her. As a result, Autumn started to awaken and shed layers of unhealthy patterns as she embarked on her healing journey. This eventually led her to channel her trauma into a new path of supporting battered women and children, helping them start new lives.

Those who awaken can see the blessings in the trauma. Autumn realized that she would not have impacted so many lives, giving women and children hope, if she hadn't lived through the trauma her parents and husband put her through. Once she forgave them, she felt free and grateful for what they taught her. She believed she incarnated in her current lifetime to learn self-love, self-worth, forgiveness, and courage. How could she have had such a profound impact if she hadn't gone through the darkness and emerged into the light? You can't have one without the other.

When Autumn explored her soul contracts, she realized that the triggers from her husband went back to childhood when she was abused physically and emotionally by her father. Her mother did little to protect her and her sister, and in this life, Autumn had the opportunity to protect Sam. Below are excerpts from Autumn's journal.

Journal Entry: September 15th

Five years ago today, the court sentenced Dean to ten years in prison for physically hurting Sammy so severely that I nearly lost my sweet girl. A day doesn't go by that I'm not riddled with guilt for putting her through that torture. She is doing so well now. I'm glad Dean is out of our lives. I fear the day he gets out of prison.

I've been putting off this exercise because I don't want to have to relive the memories. I still haven't forgiven Dean for what he did to us. How can I? Why should I? We were the victims of his cruelty and insanity. How could I have been so blind? We didn't deserve the pain and suffering he put us through. But as my therapist keeps reminding me, forgiving him doesn't justify his actions; forgiving him allows me to break free from the past and his energetic hold on us. I still struggle with that concept. I don't know that I agree with her view on forgiveness. I am still working through it.

Journal Entry: December 1st

Lately, my desire to heal and give Sam a good life is getting stronger than holding onto the past anger and living in fear. So here it goes. I have no idea if this exercise will work, but I am willing to try. The first soul contract I need to heal from the trauma is the emotional and physically abusive marriage to Dean. I looked at a photo of me from when the abuse was so severe. It's hard not to start berating myself for being so weak. I think of all the women at the shelter I've helped, and I can find a spark of compassion for myself as I recite prayers for my healing.

The emotional triggers I continue to feel are fear, hatred, anger, rage, sorrow, resentment, rejection, shame, disgust, betrayal, helplessness, vulnerability, hopelessness, hurt, insecurity, and despair. I didn't realize I still harbor so many dark emotions in my heart.

The two people in my life who triggered these emotions (characters in my soul contract) were my father and Dean. They could trigger me so quickly. I found myself being reactive. I still hold onto the victim mentality because I want them to feel the pain they inflicted on me. Because of them, I lied and became defensive and rude to others because I felt so much shame and embarrassment for enduring Dean's abuse. I was always nervous and on edge, and I deliberately made myself small and put myself down. I hated myself when I did that. I still do that at times and have to catch myself.

I'm ready to heal this part of me, but I still get triggered when someone criticizes me, looks at me crossly, or I feel they're laughing at me. I struggle with understanding why.

Journal Entry: March 1st

I've been contemplating the question of why I continue to be triggered, and I realized today that this trigger isn't solely from my marriage with Dean. It goes back to my childhood. I've done so much work to heal from the trauma I endured during my marriage. Now, I realize this trauma is much deeper. The trauma started with my father.

Dad was a cold, heartless, hateful bastard. He was always so angry at everyone and everything, especially me. He constantly shamed and berated me. He told me I would never amount to anything and that I was worthless, stupid, and a disappointment to him. When he drank, he would physically hurt me. He used his leather belt to whip me or his fist to punch me. My mother did little to protect my sister and me. I associated love with abuse because I didn't know any different. I never understood why Mom stood by so weak and allowed him to hurt us.

After Dad died, I felt relief and guilt for feeling glad he was gone. I later learned his father abused him, too. As much as I hated that man, I realized he repeated his father's behavior. I was so desperate to get away from him that I married Dean after only six months—a man just like my father. On some unconscious level, I felt I didn't deserve better.

So, what have these traumas taught me if I am to answer the question honestly? Strength because I survived. Courage to heal.

Perseverance to make a good life for Sam and me. Forgiveness, compassion, and love for myself because without going through these experiences, I wouldn't have been able to help so many women and children in the same situation. I have been and continue to be instrumental in these women's lives. To show them they have choices and the right to choose differently.

I realize now that my father and Dean fulfilled their contracts perfectly. I understand these experiences prepared me to be an inspiration to women who come through the shelter, attend my speaking engagements, and seek out my counseling. I am finally ready to forgive them both. It doesn't mean I want Dean back in my life or to commune with my father from the other side—quite the opposite. It means that I am worthy enough to have the life I desire. I will continue to dedicate my life to helping battered women and children. To give them hope, help them transform into independent, powerful, and confident individuals, and break these cycles of abuse so that it isn't passed on to the next generation.

Finally Free, Autumn.

*** * *

Now, it's time to grab your journal and favorite beverage. Let's explore your soul agreements and the characters in your soul movie. Spend some time contemplating these questions. This exercise will activate your ego, which will try to justify your reasons for remaining a victim. Put your ego in timeout while you do this exercise.

Having compassion for yourself is essential as you work through these questions. Take your time with it. There are no wrong answers. These experiences were part of your soul contract to learn valuable lessons, not a spiritual sentence to stay imprisoned. You're simply discovering where you're at on your soul journey and giving yourself permission to heal so that you can manifest the life you desire.

Exercise: The Sacred Bonds of Soul Contracts

Soul Contracts: List 1-3 experiences that significantly impacted your life.

a.
b.
c.

If you struggle with this question, ask yourself: What areas in your life need healing? In other words, what paralyzes you from moving forward into the life you desire? Who or what prevents you from making the changes that will bring you joy, peace, happiness, and overall well-being?

1. Find pictures of yourself at the ages you experienced each trauma. Select the photo from your earliest one. Study the picture with love and compassion for how far you've come. Place the picture on your heart and close your eyes. Take three deep, cleansing breaths, and recite the following prayer, "*I call upon the divine to surround me with the beautiful light of protection as I work through these memories. I ask that you give me the courage, wisdom, and guidance to answer these questions truthfully and stay in a state of compassion and love for myself. I accept the healing I need and the ability to forgive myself and others so that I may evolve to higher consciousness with ease and grace. With a grateful heart, thank you.*"

2. When you're ready, open your eyes and answer who were the characters in your soul contract based on your first trauma.

3. What role did they play?

4. What did this experience teach you?

5. Who still triggers you? Why?

6. How do you react when you're triggered? List the behaviors.

7. Do you recognize that you're giving away your power each time you react to this person? Yes/No?

8. Are you ready to heal from this experience? Yes/No?

9. If you answered no, why? Remember that the people in your life triggering the same emotions are only teachers, letting you know this experience keeps repeating because it has multiple layers.

10. If you answered yes, let's continue. You're going to write a letter to your abuser expressing all of your emotions and feelings. Don't worry about the language or words you use. If you need to cry, scream, or pound a pillow, let it out. At the end of the letter, see if you're ready to forgive them and release them into the light. Remember that forgiving them sets you free; it doesn't condone what they did. It was a soul contract you two agreed to play out in this lifetime. You may have done the same thing to them in a past life, so it isn't about judgment; it's about healing.

11. You can also receive the same impact through a visualization exercise. Visualize sitting in a comfortable chair in your sacred space. It can be a garden, by the ocean, in a forest, or whatever makes you feel safe and comfortable. Invite the person in, and ask them to sit across from you. Once they're seated, tell them you have something you'd like to share with them, and they're not permitted to talk. Once you're finished saying everything you need, ask them to leave so that you can process your emotions. If you can reach the forgiveness stage, call them back and ask them if they have a message for you. Tell them you understand you had a contract with

them, thank them for completing their end of it, tell them the contract is over, and release them into the light. If you harbor any low vibrational feelings toward them (anger, hate, revenge, shame, etc.), you must repeat this exercise until those feelings no longer control you.

12. Based on your experience, identify your soul lesson from it.

13. Repeat this exercise for each experience you listed in question one. It may take you several weeks or several months to work through these. Take as much time as you need. Your goal is to stand in your power as a warrior, not as the wounded. Allow yourself to release these toxic, debilitating emotions and accept the healing. If it feels too overwhelming, surrender it and ask God to take care of it until you're ready. This doesn't mean you get to dictate how He should handle it; it simply means you trust that He will. Ultimately, this healing helps you regain your power because you are a strong, powerful, and beautiful soul. You can do this!

CHAPTER 8

LIBERATION THROUGH FORGIVENESS: EMBRACING THE POWER OF LETTING GO

"Holding onto anger is like drinking poison and expecting your enemy to die." ~ Unknown

Julie spent two years on Martha's Vineyard working with a therapist to heal her trauma, change her belief system, and transform her life. She longed to feel peace, happiness, and freedom. She wanted to belong somewhere—anywhere. Part of her healing meant forgiving the people who had caused her suffering, especially her family.

Julie believed she had made significant progress with her therapist and considered stopping her weekly sessions until one rainy afternoon when she received the call from her father's attorney informing her of her family's tragic death in the car accident. She felt all the old feelings flood in as she struggled with deep remorse about her decision to prioritize her healing and well-being, relinquishing all contact with her family. It was another layer that Julie needed to heal—the guilt she always felt when she accomplished something for herself or, in this case, putting her needs first. This guilt was due to the shame her family had inflicted upon her. Suddenly, however, upon hearing the news, she felt alone and lost.

One afternoon, as she strolled along the ocean shore, she remembered the safe deposit box key that belonged to her father. Inside the box was the birth certificate, a photo of the baby, and the letter addressed to her father, signed "Forever yours, M."

The mother's name on the birth certificate was "Monique," and the baby's name was Juliette. Julie assumed Monique must be the "M" who signed the letter, but was the baby her? Was she the baby in the photo? She didn't think so at first, but then again, she had never seen baby pictures of herself.

After searching for answers for nearly two years, Julie found a relative she hoped was Monique's sister in a small village in Brittany, France called Rochefort-en-Terre. She traveled to France and went to the address she had found. But she had to spend several minutes before she could gather the courage to walk up the cobblestone drive to the home she hoped would have the answers to the secrets contained in the safety deposit box for more than fifty years.

When she arrived at the door, she felt her heart rate surge as she reached for the door knocker. A cast-iron skeleton key rested on a decorative lock with the initial "M" engraved above the keyhole. She knocked twice but suddenly felt so overwhelmed with anxiety that she started to walk back to her rental car. Then, the door creaked open. A tall, thin, attractive woman stood in the doorway. She looked to be in her eighties, with long gray hair resting on her shoulders and the sides drawn back with barrettes.

"Hi, my name is…"

"I know who you are, Juliette. You look just like your mother. I wondered if you'd ever find me. My name is Antoinette."

Julie's legs grew weaker, and she felt her face redden.

"Please come in," Antoinette said.

Julie walked into the beautiful parlor feeling like she was in a trance. She noticed a large baroque, gold-framed mirror hanging above an antique gold and white Louis XV French boudoir chaise.

Antoinette led Julie to a small Victorian sitting area. "How did you find me?" she asked Julie.

She told Antoinette about her family's tragic death and what she found in the safe deposit box. "I tracked you down as a relative to the name listed as the mother on the birth certificate—Monique André."

"Ah, yes, my Monique."

"Who are you?"

"I am your grandmother."

"My grandmother? You mean, Monique was your daughter . . . and my biological mother?"

"Yes. It's a long story, mon amour."

"Would you tell me?" Julie asked.

Antoinette stared at Julie intensely for several moments. "Are you sure you want to know? Sometimes, the past is best to leave buried."

"I wish everyone would stop trying to protect me. I'm a grown adult, for God's sake," Julie hissed.

Antoinette nodded and began.

"My daughter—your mother—fell in love with a man who visited the village many years ago. His name was Charles Hudson, III."

Straining to hold back the tears, Julie gasped, "That's my father!"

"Yes. I knew Charles. He was a kind man, but he was at the height of his career then. He craved power, success, and fortune," Antoinette explained. "Charles and Monique fell in love the summer of 1961. They were inseparable. I worried things were going too fast. He regularly traveled to France on business and then traveled here only to see my Monique."

Julie put her hand to her chest and took a deep breath. "My father was married to a woman in 1961, and I thought she was my mother."

"Yes. Your father had an affair with Monique. They fell deeply in love with each other. I disapproved of their affair, but their love was so pure, so intense. Many yearn to experience pure love as they had but never get a chance. They often reminded me of a lock and key. They fit perfectly together. Every time Charles left, Monique was heartbroken, though. His visits became more infrequent, and his last visit was in the summer of 1963. He came to say goodbye."

"Why?" Julie asked.

"Your mother learned of his affair and threatened to ruin his career and reputation. He was at the top of his profession. That type of scandal destroyed men like your father, especially someone with his level of power."

Julie sat quietly, processing what Antoinette had shared. She felt empathy for her father and for Monique. She longed to feel loved and in love, to have that special bond that her father and Monique shared. She never felt that with her own fiancé, so she broke off the engagement when she realized she wasn't in love with him.

"What happened after my father left?" Julie asked.

"He shattered my little girl's heart that day. But as angry as I was at him, I knew deep down that his heart was shattered, too. Then, several weeks after Charles left, Monique learned she was pregnant with you. She reached out to him, but he never answered her letters. One day, she was in town and ran into him. He was here on business, but he didn't intend to visit her. She told Charles she had tried to contact him several times and asked why he didn't respond. He said he never received her letters. He also told her he would never stop loving her but couldn't afford to lose everything he had worked so hard to build. He said he needed time and would return for her."

"So his money and status were more important than the woman he loved?" Julie asked.

"He was young and naive. He deeply regretted that decision later," Antoinette continued. "When Monique was six months pregnant, she moved to the States. She thought if Charles saw his baby—saw you—he would change his mind and want her back sooner. I forbade her to go, but she went anyway. She never came home. She was diagnosed with peripartum cardiomyopathy in her final month of pregnancy. Unfortunately, she died five months after giving birth."

Julie stared at Antoinette in disbelief. She raised her hand to her heart again, as her eyes filled with tears.

"Are you all right, mon amour? Shall I continue?" Antoinette asked quietly.

Julie looked up and nodded.

"As Monique's condition worsened, she wrote a letter to Charles, signed as M. She wrapped you up, placed you and the letter in a bassinet, and asked a friend to take you to his home. I later received an antique chest with a letter asking that I give it to you when the day came."

"My mother left me a chest?" Julie gasped.

"Yes. I believe the skeleton key she left you will open it," Antoinette said kindly.

"When Monique sent me the chest, she also sent me the door knocker with her initial as a gift and a note about how sorry she was that she broke my heart. After that, I never heard from her again. So I never got to say goodbye to my sweet girl."

Julie sat frozen in the chair. Thinking back, she realized how unhappy her father seemed and how much he drank.

"When I was growing up," she told Antoinette, "my mother—the woman who raised me—hated me. My father wasn't as cold and hateful to me, but he often said hurtful things when he looked at me. I never understood why they both were so mean to me. I never felt like I belonged in my family because, compared to me, they treated my siblings so lovingly. So I carried their disapproval of me my entire life."

Antoinette stood, walked to the mantel over the fireplace, and picked up a silver mother-of-pearl picture frame. She handed it to Julie, then returned to her chair.

"How did you get a picture of me?" Julie asked.

"That isn't you, mon amour. That's your mother, Monique."

Julie looked up in disbelief. "We look identical!"

"Yes. I believe that was partially why your father treated you the way he did. My daughter died of a broken heart. Charles chose power over love. He loved Monique deeply and lived with regret for the rest of his life."

"This explains the dark pain I always saw in his eyes. I always thought I caused the pain. I felt I disappointed him constantly, so I worked harder. But it was never enough. Now, I understand. It wasn't me disappointing him. The pain came from the constant reminder of what he lost every time he looked at me—he saw my mother in me."

"Yes. I believe you're right. It's uncanny how much you resemble your mother."

Julie stared at the picture in her hands.

Antoinette arose again from her chair. "I have something for you. Please wait here. I'll be right back."

Julie stood and walked over to the mantel to return the picture. She studied the other photos of her mother throughout the years.

"My God, I look just like you, Mom," she whispered. She felt overwhelmed with sadness, confusion, anger, and grief for herself, her mother and father, and her biological grandmother. She still had mixed feelings about the woman who raised her.

Antoinette was standing in the doorway holding a small antique chest in her hands when Julie turned around. "Juliette, this is for you. Your mother mailed it to me before she died. You have the key that fits the chest."

Julie placed her hands around the chest and delicately sat it on her lap as she lowered herself into the chair. She held the chest as if she were handling a fragile porcelain doll. She ran her fingers over the top and noticed a small, engraved dragonfly in the corner. This took her back to the day in the small bookstore on Martha's Vineyard when she bought a journal with an engraved dragonfly on the cover.

"If you don't mind, I think I'd rather open this privately," she told Antoinette.

"Not at all."

But before she left, in a soft voice, Julie asked her grandmother, "Why didn't you ever look for me?"

"I did. I contacted Charles several times, but he refused to allow me to communicate with you. I knew someday you would find me. I know this is a difficult story to hear, mon amour. But as heartbreaking as it is, I hope it brings you some closure."

Julie could see the pain in Antoinette's eyes, and in that moment, she realized her grandmother also suffered from a broken heart—all because her father decided in 1963 that his career and status were more important than the love of his life.

Julie carefully set the chest on the floor and embraced her grandmother. She could feel how frail she was. "Thank you," she whispered.

"I hope you will come back to see me," Antoinette whispered back.

"I will." Julie walked to her car, never to see her grandmother again.

The Difficulties of Forgiveness

Forgiveness is one of the hardest things to do, especially if you or a loved one is the target of a violent crime, an unfair situation, or other traumas. When coaching others about forgiveness, I'm asked repeatedly, "Why would I forgive my abuser and absolve him of his actions?"

My answer is always the same, "You're not. You forgive to release your deep wounds and toxic emotions that prevent you from living."

When you harbor deep-rooted, toxic emotions in your soul toward your abuser or a situation, you're not punishing the abuser. You're punishing yourself. When you forgive your offender, you don't exonerate them from their actions or excuse what they did. The forgiveness is not for them; it's for you so that you can set yourself free. This doesn't mean you need to engage in an exchange of conscious reciprocity. Forgiveness comes from the heart and can be done privately.

What you feel and experience is real. No one can tell you it isn't. When you suffer a trauma, you continually replay that memory and relive the traumatic event. On some level of consciousness, holding onto the trauma and emotions makes you feel that you're somehow punishing your abuser. By refusing to forgive, you feel you are hurting your abuser as much as they hurt or damaged you. But who is truly suffering? It isn't your abuser. It's you because his actions still consume you with poison that continues to harm you emotionally, psychologically, and spiritually.

The opposite of forgiveness is judgment, vengeance, and blame. As long as you hold this toxicity within you, your abuser maintains control over you because the vibrational frequency you've attached to these emotions causes a split between you and your inner alignment with your higher self—your higher consciousness. In other words, the vibrational frequency you're putting out to the universe returns to you. The universe doesn't distinguish between what you want or don't want. It can only pick up the frequency of your emotions and return more of what you're putting out. It's the universal law of attraction. This is why healing is nearly impossible when you're in survivor mode. It's a choice only you can make—to remain the wounded victim, which is disempowering and highly toxic to your well-being, or to take your power back. Taking back your power releases you from emotional hell and allows you to reclaim your freedom because your consciousness remains in the present moment, not the past or the future.

When you forgive, you release the emotional turmoil that's kept you handicapped and trapped. Hatred is poisonous to your system. The longer you replay the events in your mind, the longer you remain in a kind of prison. By no means does this diminish the injustice you experienced. Again, what you felt and continue to feel is real. The repressed emotions that keep filtering up should be respected but not keep you paralyzed in fear, anger, or shame. They shouldn't convince you that you're powerless. Forgiveness allows you to end your suffering, embrace your power, regain your life, and heal from the trauma.

Julie repressed her emotions for years, hiding behind multiple masks of pain, sorrow, low self-worth, and shame caused by her family, friends, and colleagues. She wore these masks throughout her life. As an executive in a high-powered position, she dismissed and hid her feelings.

Her position gave her power of control. She was well-trained in emotional intelligence and maintained her composure in the most stressful of situations. She used the same skills to prevent her repressed emotions from surfacing until she could no longer keep them buried deep.

Yet, Julie struggled to separate her emotions from the actual events because she replayed the same tape in her mind through the years. The more she replayed the events in her life, the longer she remained a prisoner of her emotions and believed the suffering she felt was due to the circumstances from her past. In actuality, Julie wasn't suffering emotionally from what happened in the past. She was suffering from the beliefs she formed based on the story she kept telling herself. The victim mask she wore gave her a false sense of satisfaction because it subconsciously allowed her to hold onto the blame and justify why she couldn't heal. Holding onto the blame, in her mind, punished the people in her soul contract. She didn't realize this misperception until she visited her grandmother in France.

Julie didn't open the chest until she was safely home in Martha's Vineyard. As she raised the lid, she saw an old black and white photo of her father and biological mother, yellowed around the edges. They embraced each other as Monique looked up at Julie's father.

Julie stayed awake all night reading Monique's journals, love letters from her father, and Monique's one letter to her. There was also a necklace her father had given Monique in 1961. It was a tiny, gold skeleton key with a lock. The design was exquisite, with an M engraved on the keyhole. She remembered her grandmother saying how she felt the two fit together perfectly like a lock and key.

As tears streamed down Julie's cheeks, she read her mother's letter. Monique described her undying love for Julie's father and the regret of not having the opportunity to raise her and be part of her life. She expressed how blessed she was to have met Charles and to be loved by him. Sweet emotions of love, gratitude, and passion pulled Julie deeper into the letter. Monique acknowledged the pain, confusion, and sadness Julie might feel as she examined the treasures in the chest. She asked Julie to find forgiveness in her heart and live her life to the fullest. Monique said she went to her grave loving Julie's father as much as she did the day they met, knowing that someday, the three of them would be together again.

Forgiveness. It's such a simple word, but it is so powerful that it can define or destroy our lives.

The Benefits of Forgiveness

When I started my own healing journey, I struggled with forgiveness. I remained an unconscious victim for many years. The thought of forgiving those who had caused me so much pain and turmoil seemed unspeakable. However, I longed for freedom, peace, and joy, just like the other women in this book. To experience the life you long for, a death must occur—the death of the story you have gripped so tightly. And with that death comes a rebirth.

Once you can forgive completely, your life will change radically. A sense of peace will radiate through you. You'll begin to express gratitude as your divine plan unfolds because you've released your old story and the energy attached to it. You'll have the courage and inspiration to engage in activities that bring you happiness. You'll experience synchronicities and be receptive to miracles. And you'll learn the power of loving yourself unconditionally and setting healthy boundaries.

Forgiveness removes victim consciousness and restores love because we understand our experiences are the unfoldment of our Divine Plan to heal and evolve to higher consciousness. It begins with forgiveness.

I spent years trying to heal without forgiving my abusers and wondered why my life only worsened. After I worked through the same exercises and understood the information I'm sharing with you, I reached a point where I was ready to forgive and accept the gifts my trauma brought me. How could I experience the duality of light without darkness? Love without forgiveness? Or have the perseverance to reclaim my life? The abusers fulfilled their contracts as agreed. I wouldn't be the strong, independent woman I am today if I hadn't endured these lessons. I've had many lifetimes of abuse, betrayal, and deception. In this lifetime, I agree to heal these patterns, learn to love myself, and be fearlessly authentic.

My tender, loving husband, Steve, taught me the true meaning of love, devotion, and forgiveness. He is a beacon of light and true integrity. Steve and my dear friend and devoted Self-Mastery Coach and Mentor, DyAnn, have been the teachers who taught me that embracing the richness of life experiences comes from the heart, not the mind. Living from the heart is a deeply personal and individual journey. It's about seeking authenticity, emotional connection, and a more compassionate way of relating to yourself and the world around you. It does not entail forsaking reason or logic but rather uniting them with your emotional and intuitive capabilities to guide you toward a life filled with greater fulfillment and purpose.

Now, it's your turn. Armed with the knowledge you've gathered thus far, are you ready to leave your emotional prison and thrive?

Exercise: Forgiveness and Letting Go

1. Make a list of the people you need to forgive. Do you need to forgive yourself?

2. Identify the toxic emotions that are attached to each person on your list. By holding onto these emotions, how are you limited from living the life you desire?

3. What patterns keep repeating and keep you trapped and powerless?

4. How often do you rehearse your story for others?

5. What do you hope to gain by sharing your story? Validation? Sympathy? Rehearsing your story keeps you in victim consciousness. The pain comes from what happened; the suffering comes from the labels and descriptions you attached to what happened. Once you acknowledge that this experience was part of your soul contract and you can find forgiveness, the contract is complete, and you're free. Are you ready to forgive?

6. As difficult as it may have been, what did this experience teach you? Strength? Perseverance? Self-love? By accepting that you incarnated to live through these experiences for your spiritual growth, you'll evolve to a higher consciousness once the contract is completed and released with forgiveness.

7. Reframing your story is a powerful release. This is where you shift your consciousness and return to neutrality—a vibrational state where healing occurs and transforms you to higher levels of consciousness. To do this, rewrite your story where there are no victims, only the duality of how it brought you to be exactly where you are right now—empowered to live fearlessly and authentically.

Now, we're going to conduct a burning ceremony. This ritual is one of the most powerful exercises for transformation. Through this practice, you will release your old story, belief system, and toxic emotions into the fire, allowing yourself to transform into the person you desire to be. Shamans, religious traditions, and indigenous groups worldwide have used this practice for centuries. It promotes deep healing on a soul level, helping you transform your trauma and rewrite your story to reflect the life you long for.

There are several ways to conduct this exercise. Below are four possibilities. Choose the one(s) that resonates with you most. Releasing deep-rooted emotions should be done with gentleness and great care.

Remember, it isn't about speed, but about engaging in the healing process with ease and grace. These should all be written on paper, not on an electronic device.

1. **Forgiving Others:** Write a letter to the person you need to forgive. Don't worry about grammar, spelling, or the words you choose to express your emotions. Don't judge what you're writing or how you're feeling. The intent is to transfer all of your toxic feelings onto paper to be burned and released to Mother Earth, Gaia.

2. **Forgiving Yourself:** List all toxic emotions, beliefs, or behaviors you wish to transform. These can be your feelings about yourself, beliefs, or conditions you adopted from others, or behaviors that no longer serve you.

3. **Forgiveness From Others:** List the people who need your forgiveness. You can apologize and own what you did or how you wronged them with the intention that divine light will heal the situation, releasing you both from the burden.

4. **Write a Letter:** Finally, prepare a letter or a list of what you want to bring into your life. It can simply be one word, such as peace, freedom, joy, love, worthiness, etc. You will place this in the fire after you've conducted the release portion of the ritual.

Once you have prepared your release letter or list, hold it in your hands, place it on your heart, and recite a prayer of intention. Your intention must be pure and come from a place of love, not harm. For example, *"I call upon Jesus Christ to surround me in His divine love as I release this intention into the fire of transformation. May He touch my heart, mind, and spirit and bless me with the knowledge I will take from this experience. I forgive <insert name of the person> and place them in your hands for healing. Thank you for taking this burden from me. Amen."* Place your paper into the fire and visualize the heavy emotions lifted from your heart and placed into the hands of God. Sit with that until you feel a sense of peace.

Once you feel the release, you're ready to place the second sheet in the fire for what you wish to bring into your life. As you watch it burn, express gratitude and absorb the feeling of what you placed on the sheet.

Throughout the next couple of weeks, be sure to stay hydrated and get plenty of rest. Pay close attention to synchronicities, signs, and dreams. Messages and healing can come in many forms.

Be gentle with yourself and honor what you experience.

If you don't have the means to burn your letter of intention safely, you can do the same exercise through visualization.

Remember: your past can only define you if you allow it to. When you own your story, you own the right to rewrite it and give it a new ending. Through forgiveness, you'll find freedom.

You have done a remarkable job. Show the world your beautiful, authentic self, Warrior. Own your power.

CHAPTER 9

THE PATH TO AWAKENING

"Awakening is the discovery that you were never lost; you were just asleep." ~ Anonymous

My life changed drastically during my early forties, leading into my fifties. Many labeled me as going through a mid-life crisis or criticized me for how I felt. My doctor said I was going through "the change." I remember thinking how easy it is for others to label, judge, or ridicule us when they see us struggle instead of offering compassion and support. Rather than moving straight to judgment and labeling someone as an addict or fat or weak, why can't we acknowledge the person is going through something by extending kindness and understanding instead? Why is it so easy to be careless with our words and inflict more pain on a suffering person? When it's so natural for us to place judgment and labels on others, who are we really judging? It's actually a mirror reflection of how we feel about ourselves. We put on our judgment/righteousness masks to avoid feeling our own pain and redirect our suffering onto our target with little regard for the imprint we leave on their life.

I dealt with being labeled, judged, and ridiculed my entire life. I knew I wasn't going through the change or having a mid-life crisis. I was experiencing something much deeper that I didn't understand at the time. It felt like being swept into a tornado as I watched my life fall apart. And no matter how hard I tried to gain control and make changes, nothing mattered. Instead, the experiences intensified until I was brought to my knees one final day before finally surrendering.

During this time, my husband experienced several serious illnesses. We went to multiple doctors and spent thousands of dollars, but the medical recommendations only worsened his condition. No one could seem to provide the correct diagnosis. It broke my heart to watch his decline, and I feared losing him. As a result, my own health declined significantly as well. I gained a lot of weight that I couldn't lose, no matter how hard I tried. The stress I endured since my sister's death and other events started to take a toll on me.

My relationships also changed considerably. I started pulling away from those in my inner circle who claimed to be friends but had hidden agendas. Their intentions were self-centered and manipulative. I've always been a private, quiet person who rarely revealed what I was going through. Watching their behavior was disappointing and heartbreaking, especially when I needed a friend. The same pattern was also playing out with people at work. They deliberately undermined, lied, and betrayed me. They used their titles, inflated egos, or their sense of entitlement to blame me for things I didn't do or discredit my reputation, and they lied because they felt entitled to take something from me. Their actions were deliberate, disparaging, and unethical, but they were protected because they were part of "the tribe." The more I refused to conform or play their games, the harder they made my life. I continued to tell the truth and was punished repeatedly for standing firm in my integrity. They wanted control over me. I refused to conform.

Due to all of this, I left my position, leaving a lot of money on the table. The corruption and toxic culture poisoned my soul and made me physically sick.

Isn't that what's wrong with our world today? How many join the tribe and trade their integrity because it's easier or jeopardize their values out of fear, control, power, and greed?

After years of enduring this treatment, I grew to despise my profession. The skills, knowledge, and expertise I acquired throughout my career and depended on no longer served me. What used to bring me joy and happiness suddenly brought me misery. I constantly faced hidden agendas, judgment, and criticism from people I thought cared about me, including family members, and was disappointed to learn they didn't. I felt like God shook me to the core, and when I finally caught my breath, He shook me again. It was like I was dying a slow, painful death and had nowhere to turn.

Through my life's trials and tribulations, I became a pillar of strength and was determined never to allow anyone to break me. My life hasn't been easy, but I never gave up. But my soul was tired.

To try to improve my life, I went on a quest to find answers. I tried numerous spiritual modalities, read hundreds of books, paid for alternative healings, and sought out mediums to shed a glimmer of light, hope, or direction. I prayed, begging for relief, but it seemed like the more I prayed and asked for guidance and strength, the more challenging my life became. I felt like I was under spiritual attack. And when things couldn't get any worse, I was bombarded again with more heart-wrenching experiences that took my breath away and brought me to my knees.

I started to lose my faith and my trust in God. I felt alone, stood alone, and believed no one understood. I felt trapped in my body like a caged animal, and I even thought I was losing my mind.

But was I? No, quite the opposite. I was going through what is known as the *Dark Night of the Soul*. I was slowly dying, metaphorically speaking, so that I could birth a new life. The old me that served my needs until this point in my life no longer worked. I was awakening to the person I came into this life to be, yet I couldn't awaken by holding onto the old, outdated beliefs and conditioning that dated back to my childhood. Nor could I continue the relationship with those who only cared about what they could take from me.

When you go through the Dark Night of the Soul, your perception of life changes radically. This experience forces you to surrender everything you know and are comfortable with, including your ego. When the ego feels threatened, it looks for people or circumstances to blame so that you can remain the victim. It doesn't want you to grow. It's a process of Edging God Out (EGO) of your life.

When you begin the awakening process, you experience a shift in consciousness—*Awakening the Consciousness Within*. There's no going back. Everything about you changes, and your awareness separates from your thinking. It's your soul screaming for a new life—a new beginning. You feel uncomfortable in your skin and don't understand why. You crave freedom. You start to question everything—your life purpose, values, social conditioning, relationships, career, and the decisions you've made. You begin your search for answers to questions you've kept hidden deep within your soul or were too afraid to explore.

You feel alone and alienated in the world, thinking that no one understands what you're going through, and you withdraw further into yourself. You begin to wonder if you're going crazy. As if that weren't enough, anxiety or depression creeps in, suffocating you as you start to lose hope.

So you walk away, quit your job, withdraw from society, and reduce your social circle to one or maybe two of your closest friends, if that.

You feel lost, empty, overwhelmed, and tired to the bone. Life loses its meaning. You don't know what makes you happy anymore. You lose interest in things that used to bring you joy. So, you start examining your life, beliefs, interests, and habits.

You crave quietness, nature, and aloneness. You experience an acute sense of separation from everyone and can no longer tolerate small talk. Conversations seem meaningless to you.

You become more sensitive. You may experience changes in your health that take you by surprise. And you wonder how you got so lost.

You don't know what else to do, so you make an appointment with your doctor, who provides a diagnosis followed by recommended prescriptions, depending on your age and symptoms. Several weeks pass, and you go back for a follow-up, complaining that you still aren't feeling well. They change your meds, increase the dosage, or give you more prescriptions while you continue to run in place on your hamster wheel for months, maybe years, without understanding what you're experiencing or why.

Finally, as you reach the lowest point in your life, you think God abandoned you, and you begin to lose your faith and question your religion. You become angry. You may shut God and all spiritual beings out of your life. The Dark Night of the Soul—a period when the life you're accustomed to shatters.

If only someone would have told you that you aren't losing your mind; you're undergoing a spiritual awakening. It's an emotional, mental, and spiritual death—a rebirthing process. It's when your soul is ready to go through a complete transformation. After all, the opposite of death is birth, not life.

Similar to a snake shedding its skin, life is eternal. You're merely shedding the life that no longer serves your highest purpose. You must transcend your old limiting belief systems, habits, and practices to evolve to higher consciousness and higher vibrational frequencies. It's surrendering to a higher purpose vs. staying stuck in your ego-mind of control, fear, or other crippling emotions.

Eventually, you feel more compassion, self-acceptance, self-empowerment, and self-love for yourself and others. You finally put yourself first and take accountability to change your life, disregarding all external influences, pressures, or opinions.

We do enter this world with innate wisdom, but it's easy to lose our way due to conditioning, belief patterns, and the influence of others as we navigate through life. It isn't until we experience the Dark Night of the Soul that we truly yearn for a deeper understanding of life and ourselves. It's during this crisis that our soul begins to awaken, marking the beginning of our rebirthing process.

Many life events can trigger a crisis in our lives, such as losing a home, the death of a loved one, a divorce, an affair, a fatal accident, losing a job, a chronic illness, having a baby, addiction, empty nest syndrome, a near-death experience, menopause, aging, or natural disasters. The list is endless, but regardless of the type of crisis we experience, it opens the door for us to reconnect with our true authentic self. We feel a deeper sense of peace and knowingness that the divine is in charge. It's an invitation from God, Spirit, or the Angels (whomever or whatever you believe in) to allow them to lead us on our new journey. It's called surrender.

Surrendering is letting go and living in the moment; it's about remaining present. When you surrender, you no longer feel fear or the need to control everything or everyone. By allowing divine wisdom to intercede on your behalf, you release your beliefs about what should happen, how it should happen, and when. Living in the present moment means relinquishing all control and letting blessings and synchronicities flow naturally. You no longer need to know the outcome because you trust that the divine is in charge. After all, the divine already has the blueprint for your life and your future.

Psychologist Carl Jung introduced the term "synchronicity" to characterize deeply meaningful coincidences that occur in one's life, which some refer to as miracles. These occurrences involve a sequence of symbolic events and may indicate the presence of God or angels, conveying messages or offering guidance. Here are some examples:

1. Angel Numbers: You see repeating numbers (e.g., 111, 222, 333, 444, 555, 123, etc.) consistently throughout the day on the clock, license plates, grocery bill total, etc.
2. You receive a message at the exact moment you need it.
3. You move cross-country next to a new neighbor who later becomes your spouse.
4. You're at the right place at the right time to land your dream job.

5. You take a different route to work and later learn you avoided a terrible accident.
6. A book falls off a shelf, and as you pick it up to return it, you become intrigued and decide to read it, amazed that it contains the exact answers you seek.
7. An animal crosses your path several times within a short period, and when you look up the animal's totem meaning, it validates your current state or provides gems of wisdom you need to hear.
8. Your nightly dreams become more vivid.
9. Your intuition is more profound.
10. You feel an energy around you, and you know Spirit is taking care of you.

These synchronicities are your angels (or whatever spiritual being you believe in) orchestrating the events in your life and supporting you on your journey because you've stepped aside, trusting all is well.

When you trust, you believe the events in your life are divinely guided, preparing you for the next steps during your awakening process. It may not be how you think things "should" happen, but who's to say what happens isn't better than what you had planned?

The divine is all-knowing. He sees what you don't. People often struggle with this concept because they can't see the divine. You can't see the air either, but it's there. You can't see the wind, but you can feel it. Can you imagine the freedom that comes with releasing a false sense of control, allowing yourself to live in the present moment so that you can stop waiting to enjoy life?

Faith's Dark Night of the Soul

During graduate school, one of my professors assigned a class project for which we would work with a partner. At first, I dreaded being paired with a stranger, especially since the project was thirty percent of my grade. But looking back at that experience, the universe orchestrated it by pairing me with a woman named Faith.

Forty years old, Faith was quiet but possessed a kindness that drew people into her space. I was in my thirties, introverted and shy. I didn't make friends easily. In order to avoid disappointment, criticism, and rejection, I felt it was safer not to get close to anyone. I was still carrying the negative belief about myself from the day I overheard my mother at age five.

The first day we met, Faith immediately made me feel at ease. I didn't know how to explain it then, but it seemed like she glowed as if a white translucent light surrounded her whole being. I chalked it up to the fluorescent lights in the classroom.

We worked well together. The more time we spent on the project, the stronger we bonded as friends. One evening, we were in the school library working on our project when a woman walked by holding her daughter's hand. The little girl looked about four years old, and she paused when they walked past our table, smiling at Faith. I watched the color drain from Faith's face. She stared intently at the little girl until she and her mother walked to the other side of the library.

"Faith, are you all right?" I asked.

I watched her as she strained her neck, looking again for that little girl. I waited a moment and said, "Hey, what's wrong? You look like you've seen a ghost."

Faith blinked, shook her head, and adjusted in her seat. Her voice swelled with emotion as she tried to convince herself and me that she was okay.

"I'm fine. Sorry. I'm fine," she said quietly as she stared down at her notebook.

"I don't mean to pry, but you paled pretty quickly."

She put her face in her hands, took a deep breath, and rubbed her eyes intensely.

"Listen, why don't we stop for tonight and go grab a coffee? I could use a break, too. What do you say?" I asked.

"Yeah, sure. That's a good idea," she answered.

"You must think I'm crazy," Faith said after we got our coffee.

"No, not at all. Something clearly upset you."

She smiled and tilted her head to the side as a kind, loving gesture to show her appreciation for my genuine concern.

"Three years ago, I lost my husband to pancreatic cancer. He was forty-two years old, and we were only married for five years. The day I buried him, I got a call from my daughter's pediatrician, informing me that he was concerned about her bloodwork, and he had made an appointment with a pediatric oncologist."

I was surprised by how poised Faith seemed to be as she relived her painful memories. There were no tears, no anger, and no self-pity—only sadness. She exuded a sense of peace and calm as she shared her story. She took a sip of her coffee, gently placed it on the table, and stared into her cup as if she had slipped back in time.

"She had just turned four when she started complaining about headaches and leg pains," Faith continued. "I figured it was growing pains, but I took her to her doctor for a checkup, and he suggested we run a battery of tests. We'd just arrived home from the funeral when the phone rang. I had named her Hope because I had several miscarriages, and when I finally became pregnant with her, I had a lot of complications. My husband and I feared I couldn't carry her to full term."

"I've always loved the name Hope. It's so beautiful," I interjected.

"Yes, it is. Ironically, it means a beacon of light. Hope was my beacon of light. She was beautiful, funny, and full of love and passion. I lost her to cancer one year ago today. The little girl we saw in the library could've passed for her twin."

Faith reached into her purse, pulled out a picture of Hope, and handed it to me. I felt chills run down my spine. She was right. The girl in the library looked just like Faith's little girl.

"I know she's in heaven with my husband and my father. They're all together. I still have days where a wave of grief comes out of nowhere and takes my breath away."

"I'm so sorry, Faith. I can't even begin to imagine what you went through."

"I lost my father the year my husband was diagnosed with cancer. My mother died in a car accident when I was seven. I survived, but she didn't. My father raised me. We were very close."

"Do you have family or friends who live near you?" I asked.

"No, not anymore. I had a couple of good friends, but it's funny how friends stop calling when you go through such a traumatic loss," Faith said quietly.

"So you went through all this by yourself?"

"Yes. When my husband was in stage four cancer, my boss fired me because I missed too much work. The company gave me a severance package, but it wasn't much. Then, Hope got sick, and I had to sell my house to help pay for her care. I'm still in debt, but I wanted to finish my degree. I'm only a couple of credits away from graduating. I thought it would help me get a better-paying job."

We sat for a moment in silence. "Thank you for sharing your story with me," I said. "You've been through so much loss. I would've never guessed. How did you get through it by yourself?"

"I was angry for a long time. I took my anger out on God because I blamed Him for taking my family away and leaving me with nothing. In the end, I lost everything that meant the world to me. Mark, my husband, and I were planning a big family. We lived next to my dad, who adored both Mark and Hope. Our lives were close to perfect. And, in the blink of an eye, it all changed. I kept asking myself, why me? What did I do to deserve this? Devastation consumed me when my father died. I didn't even get a chance to grieve before we got the news that Mark had stage four pancreatic cancer. The day I buried Mark, I received a call to take my sweet baby to a pediatric oncologist. A year later, I spread her ashes by her favorite tree. When I was spreading her ashes, I felt her little lips on my cheek, and I cried until I couldn't cry anymore. No one believes me when I tell them I felt her precious kiss."

"What a gift your daughter gave you. And it doesn't matter if others don't believe you. If you felt Hope's kiss on your cheek, then that's what it was."

"That's kind of you to say, but you don't need to pacify me if you think I'm crazy, too."

"I don't think you're crazy at all. I believe you. Why wouldn't I? I think you're one of the strongest women I know. I don't know that I would've been able to handle what you went through."

"I spent months feeling so lost and depressed. There were days I didn't think I would survive. I begged God to take me, too. I was at the lowest point in my life when I received a call from my old college roommate, who invited me for a visit. She lived in Sanford, Florida, right outside of Orlando. I almost didn't go. Pretending I was okay was too much to endure, but I needed something to get me out of my funk. I needed a change of scenery. Then, the strangest thing happened. My friend took me to a small historical town called Cassadaga. It's a community known as the Psychic Capital of the World."

"I've never heard of it. Did you get a reading?" I asked.

"Yes. I went to a woman who communicated with the afterlife. I never really believed in all that, but I was so desperate for answers, I figured what the hell."

"Did your family come through?" I was intrigued.

Faith smiled, and her face lit up as she put her hand over her heart, remembering the moment. "Yes! They were all together."

"How did you know the medium was genuine, if you don't mind me asking?"

"She gave me messages that only my husband and I knew. Hope told her the last words I whispered in her ear before she died. And my father told her about my pet bunny that we buried under the oak tree in the field. There's no way anyone would ever know that information."

My arms filled with goosebumps.

"The last thing she said to me is what healed me," Faith continued. "She said it was time for me to surrender the grief and anger in my heart. She said it kept me stuck as a victim and unable to move forward. She also said I couldn't feel my loved ones around me or receive messages from them because of my deep grief. That wasn't what snapped me out of my funk, though. She told me I needed to find gratitude and forgiveness because only then would I see life through God's eyes and the blessings He gave me. At first, her words stung and angered me. I wanted to lash out at her. I felt she had no idea the pain I was carrying in my heart and the injustice I had suffered. But when she placed her hand on my arm and looked into my eyes, I realized she did."

"That's a pretty bold thing to say to someone who endured so much loss in such a short period," I said cautiously.

"Her message haunted me for months. I spent a long time thinking about what she said and the courage it took her to say those words to a grieving woman. Then, one day, when I was at the cemetery placing flowers on my family's graves, I felt a calmness come over me as I stared at the names on each gravestone. I knew my family was there with me. At that moment, I realized the blessing God gave me by putting them in my life, even for a short period. How many people never experience the unconditional love I shared with each of them? I had three beautiful souls who incarnated with me. To feel the loss and sheer grief showed me that without that experience, I wouldn't have known how true love feels. That's the gift they gave me. Love. I'm not the same person I was when they were in my life. I feel as if I went through a spiritual awakening. I don't have the anger, self-pity, or victim mentality anymore. I feel compassion and love in my heart, and I strongly desire to give back to others."

"I don't know if I could ever get over the grief if I went through what you did, "I said.

Faith smiled, and I noticed the glow around her body again. "I know it's hard to understand. I also know my family wouldn't want me to stop living my life. There's a reason why they went before me. They came in to teach me the value of love and forgiveness. How can I learn that without experiencing grief and anger? Could you imagine if everyone in the world felt the love I felt and received? How different would our world be today if everyone were as blessed as I was to experience unconditional love?"

"It's remarkable that you have such a healthy perspective. Do you still struggle with crippling grief?"

"Your grief never goes away," Faith admitted. "I miss my family dearly, but I get signs from them all the time. I feel them around me. I didn't feel them at first because I was too grief-stricken and angry. I thought if I controlled my life, I would never put myself in a position to go through that kind of pain again, but I finally surrendered my need to control everything so tightly. That's when my life started to fall into place. I began experiencing synchronicities, and I knew when they were around me. I received messages."

"That's remarkable. What type of messages did you receive, if you don't mind telling me?" I asked.

"Not at all," Faith said with a warm smile. "It feels good to talk to someone who believes me. The messages were different for each. I would smell my Dad's Old Spice aftershave and his cigars. My wedding song would play on the radio, and I would feel a slight breeze blow through my hair. My husband loved to touch my hair. The TV or lights would turn on at the exact time we used to have a family movie night. I found white feathers on the floor. One night, I was sitting on the patio thinking about my dad, and a cardinal flew down and sat on the railing. My father loved cardinals. Hope loved butterflies. We would rarely see them in the backyard, so I used to take her to the butterfly museum. After she passed, my yard filled with butterflies. When I thought of my husband, I would see "1028" everywhere. That's the day we got married. I started noticing other synchronicities unrelated to my family, too, once I put my trust back into God. I started looking forward to receiving the messages. It became a game for me. I now know I'm here to make a difference, so I volunteer at the grief center. I can't do that if I hold onto my anger and remain a victim. I also know my family is guiding me. I'm so blessed," Faith said as we walked out the door to go home.

While going through my own spiritual awakening, there was a period when I questioned if I would survive it. It felt like being thrown in the middle of a tsunami, and the chances of survival were slim to none. One weekend, in particular, I went for a long walk. I had walked for over an hour when I came upon a small, white church. I climbed the stairs and realized my attire wasn't appropriate. I was wearing yoga pants, a sweatshirt, and sneakers. But I looked around and didn't see any cars in the parking lot, so I zipped up my coat to cover my sweatshirt and hoped to slip in to say a quick prayer, light a candle, and leave before anyone saw me.

I opened the large wooden door to the vestibule, and as I approached the doors that led into the church, I saw a beautiful Mother Mary statue holding baby Jesus to my left. I don't know why that statue moved me to tears, but it did. I stood there staring into Mary's eyes, marveling over the sculptor's talent to capture the expression of pure love. I prayed for her guidance, wisdom, and protection. I took a deep breath, swallowed my emotions, and quietly opened the door to see if anyone was in the church. "Thank goodness it's empty," I thought.

Walking up the aisle, I felt peace and tranquility fill my heart. The feeling overwhelmed me, and I begged for it to last. I lowered myself quietly into a pew and looked around the church, admiring the stained-glass windows, the statues, and the stunning artwork. As I said my prayers, I expressed gratitude for the time alone. Then, I heard Faith's name as if someone had whispered it into my ear. I thought about her story and made a mental note to reach out to her. It occurred to me in that moment that I, too, was being presented with gifts wrapped inside the darkness of my life. The gifts of strength, endurance, and freedom from others' opinions, judgments, and control over me—the gift of unconditional self-love.

I realized the people (teachers) in my life who intentionally brought me pain and suffering through their judgment, betrayal, lies, deception, and defamation represented their own unhealed internal demons. Their deliberate actions gave them a false sense of superiority, intending to define my self-worth and expecting that I'd accept their opinions and perspectives as my own. Their opinions were just that—opinions. And opinions aren't facts; perspectives aren't truth. All that mattered was that I refused to give my power away or be defined or controlled by anyone. They were free to think and say what they wanted about me. I didn't care anymore because I knew who I was at the soul level, and my energy could no longer align with theirs. In that moment of discovery, I thanked God for the lessons and prayed He would touch their hearts so that they could find peace and love within themselves and heal their pain. I also prayed that through their healing, may they stop inflicting their darkness on others and instead treat people with kindness, respect, and love.

Of course, going through a spiritual awakening doesn't occur just once, leaving you suddenly awakened. There are many layers. When your soul is ready to grow and evolve to the next level, it's common to go through phases of intense change. Everyone is different and has the free will to awaken or stay asleep. Some turn to addictions such as alcohol, drugs, food, extreme exercise, or other life-alternating states of consciousness, which prevent healing. That's their choice.

Although difficult at times, working through each layer brings deep healing and inner peace because you break free from the mental conditioning, control, and toxic treatment of others. You remove all the invisible masks of the multiple identities that you wore to survive. You become reborn into your true, awakened, authentic self like a phoenix rising from the ashes. Through forgiveness, you find freedom. You no longer play the victim. You're no longer the vulture staying on the ground and engaging in low vibrational survival energy. Instead, you're like the eagle who soars high in the sky and remains the observer.

Once you can expand your awareness beyond the confines of your egoic mind, shedding emotional attachments and relinquishing the victim mentality, you'll begin to discern the valuable gifts being offered to you. These gifts will pave the way for you to harmonize with the life you aspire to create.

I hold immense compassion for those who have endured or are currently navigating the dark night of the soul. It may not always be easy to perceive the blessings within such moments, but if you can shift your perspective to extend your awareness beyond yourself, delve deep into your heart, and contemplate why this is happening through you, rather than to you, you will come to realize that your life isn't unraveling; instead, it's falling into a divine alignment.

This orchestration, guided by a higher power, purposefully removes everything that no longer serves your highest good, allowing you to step into your divine purpose. Reflecting on all the heartaches I personally experienced, I wouldn't change a single moment. Without those profound experiences, I wouldn't have fulfilled my true purpose: authoring this book and becoming the person I am today. For that, I am grateful.

Exercise: Gaining Insight Through Reflection

What circumstances in your life have brought disruption, pain, or suffering? Perhaps it was the loss of a job, only to secure a position that was less physically demanding. Maybe someone departed from your life, but in their absence, you were blessed with a new circle of friends who genuinely care for you. Did you experience a divorce, only to realize that you're happier or met someone who loves and appreciates you for your true self? Did you break free from a relationship where you felt torn down, controlled, or unworthy? Or maybe you broke free from an abusive relationship only to regain your freedom?

Write about your experience in your journal. After you've finished, pause to take several deep, cleansing breaths. Close your eyes and seek insight into the valuable lessons this experience has offered you, as well as the hidden blessings it may have brought. Reflect on how these lessons and blessings have shaped and changed you.

This exercise is ineffective when clouded by emotions like hate, anger, or a sense of revenge, or when you perceive yourself as a victim. By shedding these emotions and examining the experience from the depths of your heart, you'll gradually uncover the reasons behind enduring those challenges and the concealed blessings they hold.

Isn't it time to embrace the essence of the eagle, ascending to great heights and observing without entanglement? Take a step away from what no longer nurtures your soul, and embrace your authentic self unreservedly, for you are more than enough and deserve to be free!

CHAPTER 10

THE CONSCIOUS TRUTH ABOUT THE HIDDEN EGO

"The ego seeks validation; the soul seeks liberation." ~ Anonymous

Ascending to higher consciousness is often a natural progression of ego death. It's a deconditioning and integration process. This doesn't mean you must destroy your ego; instead, you integrate it into wholeness.

When you ascend to higher consciousness, you release old belief systems, childhood conditioning, and the victim stories you've continuously shared with others. You're reborn into your true authentic self. You're comfortable with who you've become. You share your opinions honestly while respecting others' viewpoints. You set healthy boundaries, align your life with what you're passionate about, and make decisions that support your core values regardless of what others or society try to dictate.

The health of your ego determines the energetic model you follow—your ego mind or your heart mind. A healthy ego mind represents your true identity, self-esteem, and self-importance. When the ego mind aligns with your higher self, it provides you with the motivation and determination to achieve your goals, be in your power, and to love and believe in yourself.

When the ego mind isn't aligned with your spiritual growth, it creates separation from your higher consciousness, as discussed in Chapter 6. It causes you to listen to the whispers of your unconscious ego, filling your mind with fear and the mental chatter of self-doubt, low self-worth, and desperation. You hold onto your past as regret seeps into your consciousness. You long for the future, always reaching and waiting for happiness, success, or peace to somehow reach you. Your worth is based on others' opinions, societal conditioning, or culture. You may keep yourself small, believing you aren't capable or worthy. Or you may wear a mask of arrogance, feeling you need to belittle others in order to feel good about yourself. You may expect special treatment and privileges based on your title, status, or talent. You may be disrespectful to those you feel are beneath you. All this chatter is your unhealthy ego mind controlling you.

Damage to your ego can occur at various stages. Generally, it starts during childhood or when you experience trauma. When this unhealed damage remains in your psyche, it creates a significant imbalance. Instead of living life in its purest form of wholeness, the ego creates separation when it disassembles, splitting in the psyche. When this split occurs, the ego consumes you, becoming your personality. You'll exhibit intense emotions such as anger, hate, worry, anxiety, fear, despair, judgment, rage, or jealousy, operating from a low vibrational frequency. Why? Because your ego is reacting to your unhealed trauma, and it feels threatened. It looks for circumstances or people to blame to justify your behavior, as it distorts the truth. During this period, you'll hide behind multiple invisible masks of your false self, such as the Victim, Judge, Martyr, Savior, Perfectionist, Controller, etc. This allows your ego to remain in your dark shadow, preventing you from wanting to or having the courage to heal your wounds so that you can integrate into higher consciousness. When you're stuck in this ego mind, you can't discern between your false self and your authentic self.

When you live in a low vibrational frequency, choosing not to heal, your ego gains more power. It battles for position and wants control over you and others. It can become overly dominant, displaying aggressive, impulsive, overpowering, and manipulative behaviors. The ego tricks you into feeling a sense of righteousness in your demeanor by keeping you in a severely negative, energetic loop. This causes you to act in ways that deceive the person you're manipulating into your inner circle until you feel you have power over them.

I've seen this behavior multiple times. I've witnessed and been the receiver of people who portrayed an illusion of kindness, caring, and interest. They draw you into their web of deception and deliberately create confusion, domination, and control to use your energy against you. They are masters at initiating different manipulative tactics to get you to talk first, reveal your feelings, or share your experiences so that they can use your words against you in a calculated manner. They will refuse to take accountability for their treatment toward you, the experience they gave you, or how they made you feel. They may twist your words, continually interrupt, and refuse to listen. They may become hostile during the conversation and place all the blame back on you. Their body language and actions may become aggressive. Their negatively aligned ego is so strong that they're often unaware of their inappropriate behavior, but they'll do anything to gain power and control over you.

If you have someone who does this to you, take back your power. Walk away; don't engage in their darkness. When you choose not to engage, you disempower them, as well as the hold they think they have over you. *They only have power over you if you give them your power.*

The energy you put out is the energy you get back, so send them love and light. Set stronger boundaries for yourself, and remove these people from your life. Once you do this, you'll be amazed at how quickly you begin attracting people who resonate with your light and frequency.

Another way to protect your energy is through prayer. Prayer is a powerful tool to summon help from the spiritual realm—your higher self, angels, Spirit, or God (whomever or whatever you believe in). Read this prayer aloud and bask in the loving light and knowingness that you're protected. Remember, you need to ask for their help because angels won't interfere with your free will.

I call upon my higher self to align with Christ's Consciousness as I sever all contracts I've made with others in this lifetime and past lifetimes who hold the illusion that they have power over me. May I continue to see through eyes of discernment as I lovingly release those in my life who have completed their soul contracts with me and no longer align with my vibrational frequency. I'm grateful for the lessons that assisted me in reaching higher levels of consciousness. I ask for divine illumination and increased awareness to recognize and release all emotions, belief patterns, and conditioning that no longer serve my highest good. I ask Archangel Michael to bathe me in his healing light. I ask that he use his powerful sword to remove all energic cords and hooks attached to me. I ask that he engulf me in the mirrored cocoon so anyone's energy projected onto me, or which I may have inadvertently attracted toward myself, is returned to the sender with love, light, and transformation. Thank you.

Going through a deconditioning process and an ego death is part of the ascension journey. During this process, it's natural for people to leave your life so that new people who align with your vibrational frequency can enter. For those who choose not to evolve consciously, hold them in love and compassion, not judgment. Allow them the freedom to progress at their speed as they gain wisdom from their life lessons that support their spiritual growth. You're only responsible for your spiritual evolution, no one else's.

Everyone is living through their own soul journey and has the freedom to exercise free will. It's essential to remember that we've all incarnated to learn lessons for our soul growth. However, people often intervene out of loving intent, trying to protect their loved ones by taking away or averting painful events. Those painful experiences, however, may serve as vital lessons that their loved ones need to experience to advance on their soul journey. We must trust in God's plan and relinquish all control so that His plan may unfold as He intended. Interrupting it simply delays progression.

Sole vs. Soul

A negatively aligned ego mind operates from an unconscious belief system controlled by fear. It creates resistance, doubt, frustration, and insecurity, preventing you from changing and having the courage to heal. As a result, you "Edge God Out" (EGO), choosing to have God live outside you. Your ego portrays itself as your "sole." What is sole vs. soul? Sole comes from the Latin word *solus*, meaning "alone."

Soul refers to Spirit. It dwells within your consciousness, helping you align with Spirit and allowing God to live within you, not outside of you. Being in alignment with Spirit is how you communicate with God. As you allow God to operate within you, hold gratitude in your heart for His love and blessings, and trust His plan, you begin to communicate with Him and hear His guidance.

The Heart Mind

Unlike the ego mind, the heart-mind emanates love, joy, peace, and compassion. It operates at a high vibrational frequency that holds light, not darkness. When you express from this positive state of mind, you are guided by your heart rather than your ego. Living from your heart means you no longer struggle with the internal fight to hide your true identity. This internal shift allows for an expansion in your consciousness.

When you transition to this level of vibrational frequency, your awareness becomes more discerning, and you recognize the miracles from God throughout your day. It could be a smile from a stranger that gives you hope, watching a child play as you feel a strong need to add more joy and simplicity to your life, or finding gratitude when you take a moment to appreciate the beauty of nature surrounding you. The messages and the soft touch of God's presence are endless.

When you go through an ego death, you strip away layers of your outdated self-identity and years of programming that you accepted from others as the truth. Your status, possessions, safety, and values also change. You remove judgments and discover the lost part of yourself that you never felt safe showing the world or were too afraid to explore. You examine your deep desire for who you want to be, what truly matters to your soul, and what life means to you.

This transformation takes courage and unbridled trust because the ego mind breaks down, and a realignment occurs. You transition from the "Physical Aspect of Reality" to a "State of Awareness," knowing that a higher order is in charge. The "Physical Aspect of Reality" is known as living in the third-dimensional world, a polarized state operating from a negatively aligned belief system controlled by your unconscious ego. The "State of Awareness" is fourth-dimensional and is known as neutrality. You become the "Observer" of your life. The fifth-dimension is considered self-mastery, where you reach a state of unconditional love because you are aligned with Christ Consciousness. This is when you surrender, and your heart completely trusts God's plan for you, no matter how challenging your life may be. The past and future are irrelevant. Pure intention creates a new reality in the present moment.

Every thought and feeling that comes up is a choice to stay where you are or move into higher consciousness—the authentic part of yourself. Everything that happens, happens. How you interpret what happens is your new reality. Everything you do in the present moment redirects your future. You're creating your future timeline moment-to-moment and thought-by-thought. Your future is right here, right now in the present moment.

When you choose to live in the present moment, there's no separation between you and God; you operate as one. You transcend your ego and communicate directly with God. Your heart is filled with kindness, compassion, and love for yourself, your ego, and others. Your inner child, ego, and shadow receive the healing needed to integrate all parts of yourself into wholeness. You ascend to higher consciousness and hold the light for the Holy Spirit to move through you, operating as one in love, light, and wisdom.

CHAPTER 11

FEAR-LESS AUTHENTICITY

"To be yourself in a world that is constantly trying to make you something else is the greatest accomplishment." ~ Ralph Waldo Emerson

Being fearlessly authentic is one of the most challenging, courageous, and rewarding acts you can give yourself. It takes perseverance to confront the most vulnerable, toxic emotions, thoughts, and beliefs that prevent you from living the life you desire.

Fearless authenticity requires being fully engaged in the now so that you can recognize and own your emotional triggers with compassion. Then, you can identify the underlying fears causing your emotional reactions. With awareness, you can choose to move toward your authentic self when toxic emotions, beliefs, and thoughts arise.

Authenticity is part of the awakening process that strips away the ego so that your awakening can begin. It's the journey to self-acceptance and self-love. It requires a crystal-clear vision of who you are at the core. It's what YOU stand for through your words, actions, and decisions, aligning with your true identity and uncompromising core values and beliefs. It's living your passion, regardless of what others or society thinks, dictates, or expects. It's about loving yourself so deeply that it doesn't matter what the world demands from you. It's discarding all the masks you've hidden behind to be accepted, approved of, or validated.

Authentic power comes from a place of vulnerability. It allows you to show the world the person God created with no apologies. It's living from the heart, speaking your truth, respectfully sharing your opinions, and allowing others to have their opinions without judgment.

As you move toward authenticity, you'll set healthy boundaries and walk away from toxic people, relationships, and situations. You will create a life that brings pure happiness and meaning without fear. You will say no to the things you don't want or feel obligated to do and yes to the things that bring you joy and fulfillment. You'll learn to trust yourself and surrender to the flow of life as you fearlessly present your divine, genuine self to the world.

What keeps us from being fearlessly authentic? Shame and vulnerability. Shame is one of the most debilitating emotions that keep us in the shadows. We live in a society that measures our worth by stereotyping what it means to be perfect. Society dictates who we should be, how we should look, what we should eat, and how our importance is measured. These rules have been ingrained in the fabric of our families, cultures, and organizations for centuries. We believe in the programs instilled within us, thinking we must pretend to be someone we're not in order to be worthy. We become a replica of our parents or someone society deems important, powerful, or successful. Through this brainwashing and the strong need to belong, we lose our true identity. If we do risk vulnerability and show the world who we are at the core, veering away from the conditions and expectations placed upon us, we're often shamed and lured back into the folds of control.

Shame is a painful feeling of humiliating disgrace. It causes depression, anger, low self-esteem, and helplessness. When riddled with shame, we often apologize for who we are because we feel small and powerless. We constantly fear disappointing those around us, which often leads to perfectionism. And the perfectionism we strive for is an illusion that living in a state of exhaustion and high productivity defines our self-worth to others.

Guilt is often confused with shame. Although both can impact our mental health, guilt can motivate us to change our behavior because of our mistakes. Shame isn't about our mistakes; it's the feeling *we* are the mistake.

Brené Brown is renowned for her extensive research on shame, highlighting a crucial distinction between guilt and shame. According to Brown (2012), guilt is defined by its emphasis on behavior, recognizing specific actions, and admitting to having done something wrong or made a mistake. In contrast, shame centers on an internal perspective, as individuals harbor a negative self-perception, believing they are inherently flawed or a mistake.

To embrace fearless authenticity, we must let go of what people think and who we think we're "supposed" to be. The desire to be authentic, love ourselves for who we are, and create a fulfilling life is more important than fitting in and being controlled by the very people who keep us in shame. It's the courage to show vulnerability as you discover your true self.

This is why it takes great courage and perseverance to go on this journey to awaken and live your life authentically. When you do, everything will change. And that's okay. Be comfortable with being uncomfortable during this transition. Once you master fear-less authenticity, you'll experience the true essence of purpose, freedom, joy, and peace. You'll courageously step into the power of your innate quality of belonging and loving yourself unconditionally—and to hell with the rest.

Lizzie's Struggle

In Chapter 1, I began Lizzie's story, telling you about our meeting, during which she told me she was afraid for her father to learn of a secret she'd been keeping.

She and her boyfriend, Elijah, had been together since childhood. Her father was very fond of Elijah and his family, which had a legacy going back generations. They were among Mississippi's most prominent, wealthy, and powerful families.

That day in the coffee shop, Elijah was excited that they were going home for the holidays. He had planned on asking Lizzie's father's permission to marry her. He would propose to Lizzie on Christmas day when both families were together for the annual holiday gathering. Earlier that week, Lizzie's best friend was helping her pack and insisted she include her beautiful black dress, patent leather high heels, pearl necklace, and gold earrings. Lizzie pressed her friend as to why she was so insistent, and she let Elijah's plans slip. She begged Lizzie not to tell Elijah and started to cry. Lizzie, utterly shocked, told her friend she wouldn't say anything and excused herself, pretending she was late for class.

Then, she ran out of her dorm room and didn't stop running until she found herself in a small cemetery. She sat down next to a large oak tree and cried until she felt she couldn't cry anymore. She realized she could no longer hide her secret from Elijah. Lizzie's therapist had warned her of the potential consequences of living this lie. She was overwhelmed with fear, anxiety, and shame. She knew if her father found out and if the town found out she had hidden her secret of being a lesbian, she would be condemned, disowned, and shunned. She sat there, berating herself until she had an asthma attack. She reached into her bag and pulled out her inhaler.

"How am I going to tell Elijah?" she asked herself. "It's going to break his heart. I can't tell my father. If Elijah loves me, he'll understand. He'll keep my secret. I'm so stupid. How could I let this happen? I don't want everyone to hate me."

Lizzie stayed in the cemetery until the sun started to descend for the evening. She felt exhausted, deflated, scared, and ashamed. She knew she couldn't let Elijah's proposal take place over Christmas break. She felt she had to tell him after Sunday's charity event.

When I met with Lizzie for coffee, it was clear that she was terrified to go home. She revealed that she had told Elijah she wanted to break up. She convinced herself that he would understand and show compassion for the secret that had plagued her for many years. She thought they would have an amicable breakup and decide together what to tell their families. Unfortunately, it didn't go as she planned. Elijah was shocked, angry, and embarrassed. He threatened to tell her father everything.

"Have you talked to Elijah since that day in November when you broke up?" I asked.

"I've tried calling and texting several times, but he won't respond. What am I going to do, Brenda? I'm supposed to fly home tomorrow. I don't even know if Elijah is already home. Maybe I'll just call my family and tell them I have the flu."

"Lizzie, look at what this secret is doing to you. Do you really think your family would disown you?" I asked.

She looked at me with such despair that I wanted to reach over and hug her. Instead, I took her hand and said, "Isn't it time to unload your burden?"

She sat silent for a few minutes and said, "I grew up in a very controlled, disciplined, conservative Southern Baptist family. My father was the disciplinarian and set the rules for the family, even for my mother. He's been a pastor for as long as I can remember. In our Baptist church, there are different standards for men and women. The women aren't equal. Women don't have a voice in the church or the community. I have always hated that. When one of my sisters or I would voice our opinion, our father would chastise us and remind us it wasn't our place. We were expected to graduate from high school, get married, and have children. I didn't want to get married. I felt like that town suffocated me, so I had to get out. I worked hard to earn scholarship money for college. My father wasn't happy that I chose to attend college in New England, but being of legal age, he couldn't stop me, not that he didn't make my life a living hell up to the day I left. It wasn't until Elijah's father mentioned that Elijah was going to the same school that my father let up a little. But he still reminds me of 'my place' when I'm home. So you can see, I could never share my secret with anyone. I'm terrified it will get back to my dad."

"How old were you when you realized you were a lesbian," I asked.

"I was around ten or eleven. It was probably earlier, but I was so young I didn't understand what I felt."

"How did you figure it out?"

"When all my friends had crushes on the boys in our school, I didn't. I had a crush on a girl in my class," Lizzie said with a slight smile and a hint of embarrassment.

"Did she have any idea?" I inquired.

"Heavens, no! My father's sermons made it clear that being gay was sinful and that we would face damnation. It was and still is considered a disgrace against the Bible and Christ's teachings. He preached that gay people would face God's rejection on judgment day, so the church rejected them, too. To reveal you were gay in our church meant abomination. When I finally realized I was, I begged God to change me. I prayed so hard, but the feelings only intensified. So this is why I had to leave and never reveal what I am. When we had school dances, my father told me who I could go with, and it was always Elijah. We became best friends, and it was safe for me to hide behind our relationship because it kept my father off my back."

"You mentioned you were surprised that Elijah was planning on proposing to you."

"More like shocked. I mean, don't get me wrong. We had a close friendship and told each other we loved each other, but I never imagined Elijah wanted to take it to the next level. He mentioned marriage a few times, but I laughed it off and changed the subject. I didn't think he was serious. How could I have been so blind? I've made such a mess of everything, and now, my best friend hates me. I've never seen him that mad before."

"Lizzie, I'll support whatever decision you make. You know that. However, I do have a few thoughts I'd like you to think about if you're open to hearing them. If not, I respect your decision. I can see you're in turmoil right now, which breaks my heart," I said empathetically.

She looked up with tears running down her cheeks. "Thank you for not hating me. Yes, I'm open because at this point, I don't know what else to do or which way to turn."

"You've been living in the shadows to meet demands, expectations, and religious responsibilities to remain the good daughter, friend, and parishioner your entire life. Nevertheless, you're hiding behind multiple masks to maintain this persona. Your fear of being shamed and rejected by your family, friends, and community keeps you in a world of deception, which is tremendously stressful," I said cautiously.

"You don't understand, Brenda. I'll not only be shamed and ridiculed by my family and people in town, but they'll also disown me!"

"I'm not saying they won't. I'm saying you're at a critical crossroads, and you need to decide if your happiness and well-being are more important than staying in an environment among people who continue to control you through shame and fear. How many years can you hide this secret and not show the world your true authentic self? You're miserable. This secret is tearing you up inside."

"I don't know if I could face the rejection."

"God created you in perfection just as you are today. There must be a reason why. Maybe you're meant to be a spokesperson and support others. There have to be others struggling with the same thing. God has plans for all of us and the work He wants us to do. Only you can determine what that is."

"Do you think I'm a mistake?"

"Absolutely not! That's shame talking. Shame makes us feel unworthy, isolated, or flawed. People who shame us do so to make us feel powerless and keep us under their control. God doesn't make mistakes, Lizzie. I believe God loves us all the same way."

"What if I lose everyone? I would be so unhappy to lose my family and friends."

"Are you happy with your life now?" I asked softly. "I know it isn't easy, and it takes great courage to walk away and take your life back. I've done it myself. I walked away from everyone and everything and started a new life because I was tired of pretending to be someone I wasn't and living under the control of others. But I'm not trying to tell you what to do. I just want you to really think about your decisions and the changes you can make to have the life you want. Sometimes, that means walking away and starting over. Only you can decide. Whatever direction you go, I'll support you. You deserve happiness. You deserve to be freed from this burden."

We left the coffee shop with the promise that she would let me know her decision. I didn't hear from her until late Spring. We met at the park after class one afternoon, and she told me she didn't go home for Christmas, nor did Elijah. He never revealed her secret because he was too embarrassed, given his social status.

The anguish she felt from the mere idea of revealing her sexual orientation to her family, friends, and community had paralyzed her in fear. She felt powerless, isolated, discouraged, and depressed.

Lizzie finished her master's degree in fine arts and went on to get her Ph.D. She immersed herself in her career and became a very successful businesswoman. But because of the lie she carried, she felt invisible to others, and the self-alienation was crippling. As a result, she suffered from depression, anxiety, and shame, spending many years in therapy to heal her fear, self-hatred, and anger toward herself, her family, and her community.

In her mid-thirties, she married a man and had a set of twin boys. She stayed married for more than twenty-five years. Her father passed away when she was sixty-two, and her mother died nine months later. Her twins were grown by then and had lives of their own. When Lizzie turned sixty-five, she asked her husband for a divorce. Again, she feared losing her family and friends, but her desire to claim who she was and stop living under the dark cloak of lies finally outweighed her terror. Her husband, although disheartened, supported her decision. He admitted that he always suspected she was a lesbian, but he was uncomfortable bringing it up. Her sons struggled with the news and didn't talk to her for several months. Eventually, they came around to some degree, but Lizzie knew their relationship would never fully recover.

Like many of us, Lizzie realized the only way to release her feelings of shame and unworthiness, which held a tight grip on her most of her life, was to own who she was with no apologies. The longer she hid her authentic self, the more power her shame would have over her.

Brené Brown (2012) highlights that shame becomes more pronounced in the presence of secrecy, silence, and judgment. This is what Lizzie had grappled with most of her life.

According to Brown's research, a sense of unworthiness frequently precedes triggers of shame, often inherited from family dynamics. Brown (2012) identifies three common responses to shame: distancing oneself through silence and secrecy, seeking validation through people-pleasing, or engaging in a counterproductive cycle by using shame to combat shame.

Lizzie's father believed that women weren't worthy of being equal partners with men. The value they served was taking care of the family, and they were required to follow specific criteria. When they stepped out of that mold, they were shamed until they obeyed, which restricted many women from having the courage to explore and live authentically. Lizzie broke away from those controls but didn't find the courage to reveal her authentic self until after her parents died.

Your Authentic Life

To become authentic, you must set your ego mind aside, delve deep into your psyche, and explore the emotions, beliefs, and behaviors that prevent you from living authentically. You must have the courage to acknowledge your feelings of shame and vulnerability. You must own that you're worthy of living your life as your true self and refuse to allow anyone else to define you.

Living as your true authentic self means your decisions naturally align with your individual needs, desires, and core values. You no longer feel the urge to conform or seek validation from others. Instead, you warmly welcome and fully accept your true self, nurturing profound self-love and self-respect. You distance yourself from those who try to shame or control you. You feel at ease in your own skin and take pride in the person you have evolved into. You establish a deep connection with a higher power, and your soul becomes fueled by purpose. Ultimately, the most invaluable reward lies in the journey of self-discovery and embracing your true self.

Exercise: Releasing The Barriers to Fear-less Authenticity

You stand for authenticity through your words, actions, and decisions that align with your true identity and uncompromising core values, not the opinions, influence, or control of others. Let's explore some questions to discover if you live from the center of fear-less authenticity.

1. When you look in the mirror, who do you see? Someone who is the epitome of authenticity, or are you still afraid to show the world your true self?

2. Are there any areas of your life controlled by shame? If so, what are they?

3. How long has this shame controlled you? Where did the shame originate, and by whom? Did they shame you into believing you aren't worthy? Or do they continue to control your power by defining who you need to be?

4. What are your coping mechanisms? Defensiveness, avoidance, overextending yourself, lying, etc.?

5. Do you often apologize when you don't need to? Why are you apologizing? Discovering the source of these behaviors will allow you to identify the emotions causing the reaction and the reason for your response.

6. What activities, people, or situations do you avoid? Why? What do they cost you emotionally, physically, or spiritually?

7. Do you value approval more than authenticity?

8. What's preventing you from living your authentic life?

9. What situations, people, or activities create an environment where your authenticity flourishes?

10. In what environment do you feel the most comfortable and safe to express your needs and opinions openly?

11. Do you live by any established boundaries that help you stay in a state of authenticity? If so, what are they?

12. Think of someone you admire. What characteristics, values, or qualities do they embody that represent fear-less authenticity?

13. What set of core values do you refuse to compromise? For example: integrity, accountability, respect, compassion, honesty, loyalty, fairness, and trustworthiness.

14. What legacy do you want to leave behind?

15. Are you ready to be your original, genuine, authentic self?

Now comes the fun part. As you move forward with the directives in this book, you get to rewrite your story with the ending that allows you to live a fear-lessly authentic life. Refrain from judging yourself for where you are right now. Instead, congratulate yourself for your honesty, courage, and determination to love yourself so deeply that you are determined to reclaim your power!

There are more than eight billion humans on this earth and more than a hundred billion who have lived and died, but there's only one of you. Embrace your uniqueness, and rewrite your story, which showcases the person you were born to be!

CHAPTER 12

ASCENDING TO CHRIST CONSCIOUSNESS: RETURNING TO WHOLENESS

"Awakening to Christ consciousness is the journey from separation to unity." ~ Anonymous

When I decided to leave corporate to write *Courageously Authentic*, I was fully aware that I was embarking on a journey that would once again test me to my core. It would bring me challenges and experiences to reinforce the teaching principles and ensure my transition and integration aligned with my desire to ascend to Christ Consciousness—a state in which there is no duality, but only the highest form of love. It's a place where you're free from past conditioning, and your belief systems and ego no longer control you. You're in a new relationship with yourself and choose to surrender to love, not fear. It's a state of awareness where conflict doesn't exist; instead, you have unwavering faith that you're protected and provided for. You feel an overwhelming sense of peace, freedom, joy, and harmony because your mind, body, and spirit are aligned. You operate as ONE with Christ (one heart, one soul, one mind, one body, and one voice).

My passion for writing this book and inviting women to have the courage to heal, reclaim their lives, and become fearlessly authentic drove me to pursue this path. I watched too many women sacrifice their happiness, including myself, because of fear, unworthiness, and old belief systems. This conditioning told them their needs and desires weren't as important as the people they were "expected" to care for in their lives.

To encourage others to live their life of preference, I chose to heal my own heart and have self-compassion for the journey I survived, as well as the one I was about to embark on.

In the past, I chose to keep my heart closed and my life private. There were very few people I allowed in my inner circle. I felt it was safer, and I could avoid the hurt and betrayal patterns I experienced so many times before. However, knowing there would be one final test—the ultimate test from the universe—for me to finish my book, I accepted that I needed to return to wholeness. How could I return to wholeness without mastering self-love and self-awareness? How could I experience wholeness when fear gripped my heart and kept it closed? I couldn't.

With all the healing I've done in my lifetime, I avoided this universal law and thought I could work around it to protect myself. I knew unequivocally that I would find that path within me and return to wholeness.

I had just survived the Dark Night of the Soul. Then, I was about to embark on a new path that would require tenacity, perseverance, and commitment to reach the level of consciousness that required me to hold the light for Spirit to move through me, so I could use my inherent wisdom to hear my inner guidance moment to moment. Knowing this would allow me to make heartfelt decisions to shift my perception and increase my awareness of what was TRUE for me regardless of others' opinions, demands, or societal conditioning.

When I shared my plans with my Self-Mastery Coach and Mentor, DyAnn, she chuckled and said, "Oh, Brenda, when you choose to write about any higher learning topics like conscious living, you're simultaneously activating a universal request for a spiritual cleansing of outdated definitions and interpretations of your own beliefs and conditioned mindset. This is integral to the process of True Change, enabling you to return to living from your authentic self. Are you ready to embark on this deep transformation of your ego mind?"

My answer was, "My soul has an important message it wants to get out to the world, so yes, I'm ready."

As each chapter unfolded, the opportunities disguised as challenges flooded in to realign and transform my definitions and interpretations so that I could truly integrate and master the principles I was writing about.

One morning at 3:00 a.m., I sat at my old wooden writing table, contemplating titles for my last chapter. I finally settled on "Ascending to Christ Consciousness: Returning to Wholeness" when a surge of fear and anxiety flooded my body momentarily, knowing this would be the ultimate teaching to complete my book. It was the door I chose to open to align with Christ Consciousness so that I could consistently operate from a place of love and compassion.

I outlined the chapter as I did the others, but every time I sat down to write, the words wouldn't come. Weeks passed, and I stared at an empty screen as my irritation grew. And then it happened—the ultimate test that brought me to my knees. My husband, Steve, whom I love more than life itself, was nearly taken from me. He struggled for many years with his health and suffered from chronic pain.

As he got worse over the past year, we attended multiple weekly doctor appointments and were seen by top specialists; he underwent several surgeries and endured countless medical tests. He was at the lab so frequently that they knew him by name. The doctors continued to prescribe multiple prescriptions with horrific side effects. And in the end, nothing changed, and no one could provide answers or solutions.

Meanwhile, his condition continued to worsen. His weight plummeted to 150 pounds. His pain debilitated him severely, limiting his ability to perform simple everyday tasks. Yet, he never complained. Instead, he was giving up, and I knew I was running out of time.

The doctor appointments became increasingly frustrating because these highly trained professionals didn't have answers to his condition, so they prescribed more pills, ordered more tests, and told us they'd see us in a few months.

An internal fire burning inside me drove me to find the answers myself. It required me to conduct extensive hours of research to thoroughly understand multiple doctors' test results, labs, and prescriptions so that I could facilitate conversations during our appointments and uncover the mystery of what was causing him such chronic pain.

It quickly became apparent that the doctors didn't take the time to review Steve's medical history or the results of the tests prescribed by other specialists. It was a full-time job to manage his care, handle insurance discrepancies, appeal insurance denials, and make weekly calls to the billing departments because of errors in submitting insurance claims. Money was tight, the bills piled up, and my stress level was at its max. I was applying for contracting positions to work from home in order to have the flexibility to continue caring for Steve, but nothing came through.

In February, we had a follow-up appointment with his rheumatoid arthritis doctor. When the doctor entered the examination room, he smiled and informed us that Steve's bloodwork was normal. I saw my husband's body slump, and my heart broke for him. This was after months of tests, appointments, prescription changes, no sleep, and 24/7 chronic pain. And there we sat again with no answers.

The doctor admitted that he was perplexed by Steve's situation, but he didn't feel the pain was physical. He suggested hypnotherapy, saying that he was certified and would like three sessions. It was unbelievably discouraging and disappointing for Steve to be told that his condition wasn't physical even though his pain was so severe that he could barely function. When I looked at him, I saw an hourglass instead, with sand passing through it at a speed I couldn't stop. Intense angst pierced through my body.

We respected this doctor as he was the only one who explored numerous alternative possibilities and worked closely with us to try and solve Steve's crippling pain. The doctor experimented with different dosages of prescriptions and ultimately referred us to the Pain Management Center in Hartford, Connecticut.

Steve also underwent the hypnotherapy sessions, but to no avail. We met with the rheumatoid arthritis doctor several times after the therapy sessions, and he adjusted the medication again to lessen the pain. Still, nothing worked.

Before our visit in May, I received a call from the Pain Management Center, informing us they weren't accepting new patients. When I turned to tell Steve, I realized he had overheard the conversation. I saw despair flood his face and knew I was out of time. The hourglass dropped the last particle of sand.

Yet, we kept our appointment with the rheumatoid arthritis doctor. When Steve finished providing a quick update, we sat there in silence. We could see how disheartened the doctor was that he didn't have a solution for us. I asked if he could prescribe something stronger for Steve to give him some relief. He prescribed morphine.

It was a quiet ride home from the doctor's office. After twenty-nine years with the man who was my soulmate and my best friend, it was the first time I ever saw him give up. When we got home, he slowly lowered himself into a chair, looked at me, and started crying. I knew what he was thinking but wasn't ready to tell me.

Later that afternoon, I drove to the pharmacy to pick up the morphine prescription when DyAnn called and asked how Steve was doing. She could feel my energy and hear the despair in my voice as I relayed the details. She was quiet momentarily, and with tenderness, she said, "Brenda, you must let him go. It's his decision if he wants to live or die. You have to respect his decision. He's waiting for you to give him permission to go." We finished our conversation, and I thanked her for her feedback. I picked up the prescription and drove home. I was so numb and exhausted that I couldn't stop, or I knew I'd fall apart.

When I walked into the house, it was eerily quiet. Fear rushed through me as I quietly walked from room to room to find Steve. He was lying on the bed with his hands folded over his chest. I stood frozen, clutching the prescription bag, and thought, "This is it. Just like Mom, I didn't get to say goodbye." I called his name, but he didn't move. I walked over to him, placed my hand on his shoulder, and he opened his eyes. I was so relieved that I nearly burst into tears but swallowed them back instead. All I could say was, "I have your prescription. Let's take one."

I left the bedroom, entered my office, and sat down. I was emotionally, physically, and spiritually depleted. I realized his doctor was right—the medical model couldn't cure Steve's condition. I also knew the morphine wouldn't relieve his pain, which was the result of unresolved, unhealed, deep-seated emotional trauma. But I didn't know how to deliver this news to him, especially after he had no relief from the hypnotherapy sessions.

As I sat there replaying DyAnn's words in my head, it was as if someone had hit me between the eyes. At that moment, I realized this was my ultimate test—surrendering to Steve's decision to live or die.

After a year of controlling every angle of the medical model, hours of research, doctor's appointments, surgeries, medical procedures, countless blood tests, and overall management and coordination of insurance, scheduling, etc. (in addition to waking up at 3:00 a.m. to work on my business plan, marketing launch strategy, design a schematic for my website, try to write, and apply for contracting jobs), I couldn't get ahead no matter how hard I tried. I always took one step forward before being catapulted back to the starting line. I never stopped to examine why. I just kept climbing over the hurdles and taking different directions. I was breaking one of the most important universal laws to living in Christ Consciousness—surrender.

When we surrender, we have unwavering trust in God's plan. We accept He's in charge and refrain from controlling the outcome. We step aside and allow His plan to unfold in His Divine timing, not ours.

Intellectually, I understood this principle, but my anger surged because the only way out was to release my husband and accept his decision regardless of the outcome. I became discouraged because my ego mind was working overtime to regain control and instill fear in me. Fear that I would lose my best friend and live my life without him. Fear that I'd never finish my book. Fear that I wouldn't be able to fund my business. Fear about paying the bills. The internal chatter was overpowering me. I quickly recognized how fast I was spiraling out of control. I took a deep breath and reinforced the spiritual principles I've studied and used for years to return to calm and regain my center.

The thought of losing Steve was the hardest thing I'd ever surrendered to. I'm not one to cry or become emotional, but when I realized this was the ultimate test I had to succumb to, I sat at my writing table holding my head as despair swept through every cell of my body. I cried tears of sadness, defeat, and exhaustion.

The next day, Steve had the worst day he ever had. Standing in the kitchen preparing lunch, I heard, "It's time, Brenda." And I realized what I needed to do. I walked into my office, where Steve was resting in a chair. I sat across from him. I acknowledged his courage over the past year and everything he endured while never complaining. I admitted his will to continue was becoming too difficult for him. I told him how much I loved and admired him and knew he had been grappling with a decision. His eyes filled with tears as he listened to me. I paused for a moment to regain my composure. I smiled and said, "I understand and will accept your decision." Steve looked at me with deep sadness in his eyes and said, "I can't do this anymore, Brenda. I love you so much and don't want to leave you, but I can't live with this pain anymore." I nodded, and with that, he kissed me on the forehead and went to the bedroom to lie down.

I put our lunches in the refrigerator and went upstairs to my writing room. I sat there, completely overwhelmed with grief. I looked around my room at the posterboards that lined the walls, holding hundreds of post-it notes for each chapter of my book, binders stuffed full of information, and research books scattered around the room. Then, my eyes landed on a large four-inch white binder that held my manuscript. I instantly found myself bargaining with God. I told Him I'd burn my manuscript and never complete my life's mission if He would rescind this last lesson. And just as fast as that thought flooded my mind, I remembered my commitment to God when I embarked on this journey two years prior. It was then that I finally surrendered and accepted that if this were His plan to bring Steve home, I would survive just like all the other times.

The following day, I received a call from DyAnn. She told me she had dinner with a shaman and asked the shaman to help Steve. The shaman agreed to perform remote healing if Steve would surrender and accept it. I thought, "There's that word again. *Surrender*." I immediately knew she was the answer. However, given Steve's state of mind, I didn't know if he would be open to this alternative form of healing. He didn't receive the full benefits from the hypnotherapy sessions because he didn't believe they would work. I released my need to control, persuade, or force this decision on him and decided I would present it as an option for him to consider.

I had followed shamanism for many years and understood the ancient wisdom behind its teachings and healing practices. The shaman's ability to heal and transform the body on a soul level always amazed me.

I found Steve sitting in the rocking chair on the front porch. I sat down and asked God to grace me with His wisdom, words, and the ability to share this information with Steve so that he could make the decision he felt was best for him, not for me. He listened without interrupting. When I was done, he turned to me and said, "The morphine isn't working. I want to try the shamanic healing." He went on to tell me that when he was lying in bed, he had a life review and forgave all the people in his life who wronged him. And he forgave himself. Then, he told God he was ready to go. At that moment, a peace flowed through him, and he knew he had made the right decision. He shared that he didn't know how he knew, but he realized the medical model wouldn't be able to heal him. He knew his healing needed to occur on a much deeper level, which was why he was open to receiving healing from the shaman.

When I walked away to make arrangements with the shaman, I shook my head in amazement that everything was falling into place so smoothly. Then, I realized it was after both of us surrendered to God's will.

God waited patiently for over a year as my need to control outweighed my ability to hear His guidance. I held onto the reins so tightly through fear and desperation that I didn't realize He was always there. Yet, the lessons over the past year were essential for both of us. For Steve, it brought him to a spiritual awakening. For me, it taught me a vital lesson about the true nature of Christ Consciousness.

The shaman worked on Steve for ten days. During his healing journey, Steve experienced remarkable insights. While he slept, his dreams were vivid, active, and full of color. He understood that deep healing occurred while he slept. This is common because while you're in a dream state, the ego dissolves, which allows for miracles.

During these healings, Steve felt a significant shift in his psyche. His pain decreased by 90 percent, his energy level increased, he regained the weight he lost, he released old thought patterns, and his desire to live returned. This experience put him on a new trajectory, and he wanted to understand how to use his inherent wisdom to heal his mind, body, and soul. So he started working with DyAnn. The transformation was so profound that it completely changed him on multiple levels. It was as if he was reborn into the person he was born to be.

During one of the shamanic treatments, the shaman shared that she saw that Steve and I had multiple lifetimes together. In one of those lives, Steve was a general in the Army who was killed during a war. I was his wife. When I received the news that he was killed during battle, I was heartbroken and never recovered from his death. This explained my unshakable fear when I had to surrender to his decision. It was a memory implanted from a past life of the terrible heartbreak I felt from losing him and not having any control over saving his life in this lifetime.

In the second lifetime the shaman shared with me, I was a great warrior, and Steve was my slave. She told me I severely beat his upper body as he walked beside me while I rode a white horse. The exact location of the chronic pain he was experiencing in this lifetime was where the beatings took place. During the same healing, I was shown a vision of Steve as my slave. My heart broke when I saw his bloody, beaten body constrained in chains. In my mind's eye, I got off my horse, unlocked the metal cuffs around his wrists, and removed the chains from his body. I took a cloth and wiped the blood from his face and arms. I asked him to forgive me, handed him the reins to my horse, and freed him. After the healing, Steve told me that he felt a sharp pain around his shoulders that penetrated through the center of his chest. He said the pain was so intense that he had to sit up straight and then lean over. After the healing session, however, his pain was gone, and I shared my vision with him.

This was a powerful awakening experience for both of us. I prepared myself by surrendering to his soul's highest order and stepping out of the way to allow Spirit to orchestrate the best possibilities and outcomes. This experience taught me to understand the power of Christ Consciousness through surrender, trust, and accepting God's will.

At age seventy, Steve allowed Christ into his heart for the first time. This experience also gave him an understanding of how he could heal himself through his own inherent wisdom.

Developing Christ Consciousness

Christ Consciousness is the highest form of intellectual development and emotional maturity. It's the state of consciousness in which we find self-realization and are one with God.

Evolving into Christ Consciousness requires accountability and ownership to embody the wisdom and to harmonize and increase our ability to respond to life experiences vs. reacting. This is paramount to why discernment is necessary. It helps to determine if we're operating from our ego consciousness (third-dimensional state of being of fear, judgment, and control) or our heart consciousness (fifth-dimensional state of love and compassion).

When we operate from the third dimension—a polarized state—we replay the old trauma to win the fight because we're in survival mode. This keeps us in the *process* of low vibrational frequency and creates a separation of higher consciousness by design.

The fifth dimension is non-physical. It is Spirit or life force, also called God's energy source. It's the soul's highest frequency, which translates as unconditional love.

Living in the third-dimensional reality, we view life through our filters (i.e., limiting belief systems), which are human definitions we apply to mask our fear. Unconditional love, however, transforms fear and our need to seek validation from others. It provides us with awareness of the need to integrate the INVISIBLE masks we hide behind as we evolve to a higher frequency. This allows our knowingness to surface within us, and the realization of living in love for ourselves and others unfolds naturally. The desire to control people or situations disappears because it's no longer relevant.

It's common to move between the third and fifth dimensions. The art of self-mastery is to live in the third-dimensional reality but practice fifth-dimensional principles by trusting in our higher self and having the conviction to believe and have unwavering faith in the unseen. This moves our frequency to a higher dimension, where the magic happens, and synchronicities unfold.

When Steve allowed Christ to enter his heart and surrender to the outcome, he transitioned from the third-dimensional reality to the fifth dimension. That's when he experienced his miracle, and his chronic pain was healed.

We've reincarnated in this lifetime to learn how to return to our true selves. The only way back to our true selves is through our life experiences. Self-mastery is the art of living in heart consciousness. You remain in the present moment. The past no longer controls you, and the future is now.

Everything you choose in the now moment is your future. You acknowledge that your suffering was necessary for your spiritual transformation and ascension to higher consciousness. As you ascend, you experience changes to your physical body because you're radiating at a very high light frequency. You'll be more acute to what your mind, body, and soul need, which becomes your top priority.

Developing Christ Consciousness requires consistent awareness and practice. There are many ways you can integrate this into your daily routine. For instance:

- You develop a strong desire to be in a relationship with God and trust in His plan through surrendering, especially when your life is complicated.
- You engage in the power of prayer to open the door to the mysterious forces of Grace by praying for yourself, our world, and those who brought you pain and suffering.
- You practice daily meditation to release fear, judgment, anxiety, or other low vibrational emotions. Ask yourself during these times, "Am I operating from heart consciousness or ego consciousness?" If you aren't aligned with your heart, hand it to God for transmutation, and send love and light to your abuser. It's only through forgiveness and self-acceptance that you free yourself.
- You practice gratitude and recite affirmations, which are powerful mantras that can return you to your center, realign your energy, and increase your vibrational frequency.
- You perform daily spiritual practices of joy, love, forgiveness, peace, calm, and self-care.
- You deepen your love and compassion for yourself and others.

- You're aware that energy follows thought and that where you place your awareness becomes your feeling state and manifests into reality.
- You read scriptures or connect to spiritual articles from your favorite blogger.

There are many other spiritual practices you can incorporate into your daily routine. Find what resonates the most with you to keep you aligned with Christ Consciousness.

As I complete this final chapter, I hope that as you immersed yourself in the stories, principles, practices, and exercises, you found deep compassion, pride, and love for yourself. As you look in the mirror, recognize the beautiful soul staring back at you, and be proud of all you've accomplished—all the masks you've discarded to reveal your true self.

It takes great courage and perseverance to embark on a spiritual journey and ascend to higher consciousness. The mere fact that you've completed this book indicates that you're ready to stop surviving and start thriving. You have everything you need inside you to attain the life you desire.

You can do it just like the women in this book, who reclaimed their lives with one decision, one step, and one action at a time. It's your time now to allow miracles to unfold as you advance on the ascension process and integrate into Christ Consciousness—the purest form of love.

You are a remarkable person. It's time to show the world how fearlessly authentic you are.

About the Author

Brenda Hukel, MBA, dedicated 30 years to Human Resources and Organizational Development before leaving her executive position to pursue a lifelong dream: empowering women worldwide to confront their fears, reclaim their lives, and rewrite their stories.

Throughout her career, Brenda witnessed how fear paralyzed many due to unhealed trauma, ingrained belief systems, childhood conditioning, and societal and cultural demands. She saw women devote their lives to their families, careers, partners, and children—prioritizing others' needs over their own. Many experienced unfulfillment and a deep longing to rediscover their passion, purpose, and happiness but didn't know how to regain it.

Brenda has coached thousands, witnessing remarkable transformations through the tools, principles, and spiritual practices she shares in her book. Today, she continues this mission as a women's speaker and advocate for transformational healing and empowerment—inspiring audiences to reconnect with their truth and take the first courageous step toward wholeness.

By sharing her own journey and those of the women she has coached, Brenda invites others to embark on a spiritual journey of awakening, enabling them to reclaim their true selves and become who they were born to be—*Courageously Authentic*.

Brenda lives in Connecticut with her husband, Steve.

Brenda L Hukel
P.O. Box 96, Broad Brook, CT 06016
Website: www.BrendaHukel.com
hello@brendahukel.com

As you turn the final page, I want to thank you for walking this path with me. *Courageously Authentic* was born from a deep desire to help women like you rediscover the truth and power within.

I hope this book has inspired, challenged, or empowered you to embrace your authentic self.

Every reader's journey is unique, and if you feel called to share yours, I would be deeply grateful if you'd consider leaving a review on Amazon or Barnes & Noble. Your feedback not only means the world to me—it also helps guide other women toward their own transformation.

Sometimes, a single shared experience becomes the spark that lights another woman's way.

Let's continue rising together. If you'd like to stay connected and receive inspiration, updates, and new releases, I'd love for you to join me on social media.

There is strength in sisterhood—and in every woman who dares to live courageously authentic.

With heartfelt gratitude,
Brenda

Social Media Accounts

- https://www.linkedin.com/in/brenda-hukel-mba/
- https://www.facebook.com/brenda.hukel
- https://www.facebook.com/brendahukelauthor/
- https://www.instagram.com/hukelbrenda/
- https://www.pinterest.com/hukelbrenda/
- @brendahukel5531

References

Bravata, Dena M et al. "Prevalence, Predictors, and Treatment of Impostor Syndrome: a Systematic Review." *Journal of General Internal Medicine*, vol. 35,4 (2020). https://www.ncbi.nlm.nih.gov/pmc/articles/PMC7174434/.

Brown, B. "The Power of Vulnerability: Teachings of Authenticity, Connection, and Courage." Sounds True Live Lecture, first published in 2012. https://www.barnesandnoble.com/w/the-power-of-vulnerability-bren-brown/1131430669?ean=9781604078589.

Clance, Pauline R. and Suzanne A. Imes. "The Impostor Phenomenon in High Achieving Women: Dynamics and Therapeutic Intervention." *Psychotherapy, Theory, Research and Practice* 15, no. 3 (1978). https://mpowir.org/wp-content/uploads/2010/02/Download-IP-in-High-Achieving-Women.pdf.

Clance, P.R. 1985. *The Impostor Phenomenon: When Success Makes You Feel Like a Fake*. 20-22. Toronto: Bantam Books.

Hay, Louise. 1984. *You Can Heal Your Body*. Hay House.

Rao, T.S.S., Asha, M.R., Jagannatha Rao, K.S., & Vasudevaraju, P. The Biochemistry of Belief. *Indian Journal of Psychiatry*, 51(4) (2009): 239–241. doi:10.4103/0019-5545.58285, https://www.ncbi.nlm.nih.gov/pmc/articles/PMC2802367/.

Sakulku, J. "The Impostor Phenomenon." *The Journal of Behavioral Science* 6(1) (2011): 75–97. https://doi.org/10.14456/ijbs.2011.6.

Schulz, Irene. "The Masks We Wear – Impostor Syndrome." *Illuminated Pathway*. 2024.

REFERENCES

Tolle, Eckhart. 2005. *A New Earth: Awakening to Your Life Purpose.* New York: Penguin Publishing Group.

Young, Valerie. 2011. "The Competence Rule Book for Mere Mortals." *The Secret Thoughts of Successful Women.* Crown Currency.

Resources

A Course in Miracles. Combined volume, 3rd ed. Foundation for Inner Peace, 2007. https://acim.org/.

Browne, S., & Harrison, L. June 2005. *Past Lives, Future Healing: A Psychic Reveals the Secrets to Good Health and Great Relationships.* Highbridge Audio.

Chopra, D., MD. 2006. *Life After Death: The Burden of Proof.* Harmony Books.

Chopra, D., MD. 2012. *Life After Death.* Harmony Books.

Dyer, W. W. 1995. *Your Sacred Self.* 176-188. Harper Collins.

Dyer, W. W. 2001. *There's a Spiritual Solution to Every Problem.* HarperCollins Publishers.

Kets de Vries, Manfred. F. R. "Are You a Victim of the Victim Syndrome?" Working Paper. INSEAD Working Paper No. 2012/70/EFE. (2012). https://papers.ssrn.com/sol3/papers.cfm?abstract_id=2116238.

Leininger, B., Leininger, A., & Gross, K. 2009. *Soul Survivor: The Reincarnation of a World War II Fighter Pilot.* Grand Central Publishing.

Newton, M., Ph.D. 1994. *Journey of Souls: Case Studies of Life Between Lives.* Llewellyn Publications.

Roman, S. 1992. *Spiritual Growth: Being Your Higher Self.* Earth Life Series, Book 3. HJ Kramer.

Roman, S. 2011. *Living with Joy: Keys to Personal Power and Spiritual Transformation.* Earth Life Series, Book 1. HJ Kramer.

Ruiz Jr., D. M. 2016. *The Mastery of Self.* Hierophant Publishing.

Ruiz, D. M. A. and Mills, J. 2004. *The Voice of Knowledge: A Practical Guide to Inner Peace.* Amber-Allen Publishing, Inc.

Shefali, D. 2021. *A Radical Awakening.* HarperOne.

Shinn, F. S. 2003. *The Complete Writings of Florence Scovel Shinn for Women.* DeVorss & Company.

Singer, M. A. 2007. *The Untethered Soul: The Journey Beyond Yourself.* New Harbinger Publications and Noetic Books.

Taylor, S. 2017. *The LEAP: The Psychology of Spiritual Awakening.* New World Library.

Tolle, E. 1997. *The Power of Now.* Namaste Publishing.

van Warmerdam, G. 2014. *MindWorks: A Practical Guide for Changing Thoughts, Beliefs, and Emotional Reactions.* 4-8, 13, 16, 21-25. Cairn Publishing.

Walsch, N. D. 1995. *Conversations with God, Book One.* Great Britain: Hodder & Stoughton.

Walsch, N. D. 1997, 1999. *Conversations with God, Book 2.* Hampton Roads. Great Britain: Hodder and Stoughton.

Walsch, N. D. 1998, 1999. *Conversations with God, Book 3.* Hampton Roads. Great Britain: Hodder and Stoughton.

Walsch, N. D. 2017, 2018. *Conversations with God, Book 4.* United Kingdom: Watkins Publishing; New York: Rainbow Ridge Books.

Weiss, B. L., M.D. 1998. *Many Lives, Many Masters.* Touchstone by Simon & Schuster.

Weiss, B. L., M.D. 2004. *Same Soul, Many Bodies.* Simon & Schuster.